# Remember

## Reincarnation Astrology

Ahura Sevgi Alis Yildirim

New York City Books

**Remember Reincarnation Astrology**
Yildirim, Ahura Sevgi Alis
Copyright ©2021, New York City Books
*All Rights Reserved*
Including the right of reproduction in whole or in part in any form.

A part of this publication may be referred with the written permission of New York City Books.

Published by New York City Books
www.nycitybooks.com

**Translator** Mehlika Özge Esirgen
**Cover Design** Alper Tornacı

**Author Contact** sevgialisyildirim@aenbibooks.com
**AARAD Society** www.aenbibooks.com

New York City Books
**ISBN:** 978-1-0879-8572-5
Published September 2021

*To Pythagoras,*
*the unquenchable light of humanity...*

# TABLE OF CONTENTS

## ACKNOWLEDGMENT ...*7*

## FOREWORD ...*10*

## CHAPTER I ...*17*

## TIMES OF REMEMBERING ...*37*
- Remembering According to the Moon Phases...*38*
- The Skill of Using Retrograde Periods of Planets to Remember Past Lives...52
- The Retrograde and Remembering...56
- Dreams of Remembering...76

## CHAPTER II ...*79*

## GATES ...*124*
- Retrograde and Direct Gates ...*124*
- 0°-29° Gates ...*158*
- Main Gate ...*161*
- Memories Activated in Decanates ...*169*
- Moon Meditation and Meditation of the Nines ...*170*

## STORY OF THE SOUL ...*185*
- Gates and Their Significance ...*199*

## CHAPTER III ...*225*

## SATURN ...*226*
## PLUTO AND SATURN ...*235*
- Finding the Soul's Planet of Incarnation ...*240*

## AFTERWORD ...*251*
## Conclusion:
- Our Fabulous "Alternative Creation" Story ...*252*

## DICTIONARY ...*265*

*Remember*

## ACKNOWLEDGMENT

The book you hold in your hands, Remember, is the result of my years of learning Hermetic astrology and applying it to my life with my valued teacher and advisor Aleksandar Imsiragic. As I will be expressing in my book, I have no intention of defending the validity or invalidity of reincarnation. My main purpose in writing the book is to make use of the language of mythology, alchemy and astrology our ancestors had used by showing how they perceived the cycle of birth and death thousands of years ago. In doing so, I would like to open a window from the past, into the present. In this way, I feel the happiness of contributing to the study of karma and reincarnation, which are fields of study of astrology, by astrologers in a deeper way. Therefore, it turns out that Remember is a textbook in the field of reincarnation and karma. I belive that one who cannot comprehend her past cannot fully give a meaning to her present. I would very much like you to know my team, who made a unique contribution to my journey of realization of this pre-supposition.

**Sociologist Ahura Sevgi Alis Yıldırım**

*Remember*

*Ahura Sevgi Alis Yıldırım*

*"Man is a memory
that has to remember himself."*

**Remember**

## FOREWORD

I have been mainly interested in two approaches of the philosophers and scientists in history of social thought as well as history of philosophy while I was continuing my sociology major: trying to comprehend an experience through understanding & trying to explain an experience through experiment and observation. There are two edge points our species have reached to make a cause and effect connection for we have gone through in our adventure of civilization. As a sociologist I have observed in psychology, anthropology, social psychology and sociology that the greatest function of science was to transform the tension of death for our species. Through various ways, the social science continuously and regularly helps us to produce different tools to transform the tension our species experience in the face of death. Once we observe in a deeper way, we see that we want to find a way to live longer and strive to survive in each breath. We should understand that we do these to comfort that part of ours that is afraid of death. I remember a meaningful sentence I heard from my brother, whose sun and ascendant are in Scorpio, on a day that we lost a loved one: *"Life is built on death."*. Therefore, science is a means of condolence for death. If you see our species through my lenses, you will see a reference point at a bottom line where our inventions are based on, which shows us that our inventions intend to cure our tension of death.

We know that the fundamental necessity of the man, who laid the foundations of civilized relationships by settling in caves, is to meet his physical needs and his need for safety. Sociologists say that man's need for safety finally gave birth to a huge organizational system called society. The need for safety has been the main reference point for the establishment of the organization we today call family. Therefore, the reference point of family is human's need for safety. We meet our need of safety by establishing families. As you see, even the act of creating a family itself is a "transformer" of the tension of death. If you read some sociological research, you probably have noticed that sociology is concerned about how people come together, organize themselves as well as the formation, structuring, progress and maintenance of the society. I believe the most profound point we can discover can only be achieved through understanding the 'family' which is the nucleus of society. Living as a society definetly satisfies the need for safety of our species and minimizes the tension of death. Feeling safe is as primary as eating, drinking and finding shelter for human beings. Society will continue to exist as long as humans fear death.

You can observe that all the written, oral, official or traditional structuring in the society are means that are introduced in the cases where one threatens the safety of another.

***It can be stated that all the social rules and values arise from the fear-based relationship that our species have developed with the concept of death.*** Could the fear of death really be the fundamental feeling which the civilization is built on? Could it be true that humanity has established tremendous civilizations just to feel safe?

Why did I feel the need to write such an introduction for my book, which is about reincarnation and explains the process of reincarnation by using Astrology, one of the most influential fields of ancient philosophy?

My main reason to write this book on reincarnation is to help people transform their tension of death. And I don't feel the need to debate about the basis of my assertive sentences above because this is not a book of sociological discussion. Nevertheless, I feel that writing a book which highlights that people can transform their tension of death into peace can help them in an effective way. The purpose of this book is nothing but helping you.

The main thesis of reincarnation is hidden in the following sentence; "Dying is transformation". It is only a process of transformation that you are exposed to. I am not writing this book for those who believe in reincarnation or others who do not. Because it is a not process that exists or not because of your beliefs. And I am not writing it for the curious either; because there are already many valuable books written for this purpose. I am writing this book for a very simple and clear purpose that is easy to understand. It is helping people to transform their tension of death. That's all.

Reincarnation means "being re-born" by definition. Some approaches regarding reincarnation highlight that only the body can reincarnate and the soul cannot; while others state that only a part of the soul reincarnates. In this book, I will state that both the body and the metaphor called soul- yes, both- can incarnate. I explain how, where and through which stages the soul is attracted to Earth's energy field as well as how the body becomes activated on Earth by passing through a specific field and how it is formed on Earth. I explain that the soul and the body incarnate in different spaces and processes that are unique to them. The soul and the body are beings independent from one another and their imminent dance begins when the influence of duality comes into play. They unite for a purpose. The reincarnation process itself means duality. The reincarnation process is the most encouraging transformation. Reincarnation process signifies proceeding towards what is new with the help of the power of transformation. The main purpose of reincarnation process is to produce the energy that is necessary to sustain the reincarnation cycle. The purpose of humans' existence is to produce the energy that is necessary for other beings to continue their incarnation processes. The human being is a source of energy. The energy of thought helps not only our planet Earth but also the incarnation of other beings on other planets.

*Human being is a source of energy that is necessary for the whole universe. As you read this book, you will realize that you, as humans, are not abandoned, forgotten and forsaken beings that were thrown here. Man is the will of the Earth and sky.* If you humans do not exist, then none of the planets or beings, that continue their existence through your energy can exist and continue their incarnation process. And the time will cease to exist the way we know it. None of the Gods or Goddesses mentioned in mythology have created you. You are a will. You are a reaction. You are a consequence that arises from the combination of secrets. We call the ones who learn and control these secrets as Gods and Goddesses. That is to say, a God or Goddess can, at the most, know the combination of the secrets that you were born from. Yet they can't create you from scratch. I invite you to see the great mystery behind the fact that gods control humans, from this perspective. Zeus or Saturn did not create you. They only know how you came into being through the composition of certain secrets. That is why they have the might to control you. In the end, you are a reason for another being's incarnation. ***Human is the will of earth and sky.***

The universe has evoked all the relevant potentialities since the time of the first sound, untill the time it reached you. This has happened for an unknown amount of time and finally the universe reached human. The aim of the universe is to activate thinking. If you observe the Gods and Goddesses in mythology, you will see that each of them has at least an expertise field and none of them creates himself/herself. It is only that the ones who hold the secrets of the stages of manifestation are declared as Gods or Goddesses. For example, Pluto is called "Hades, the god of death". We should correct this. We should say: Pluton is Hades and has been declared as a God. Because he has learnt THE SECRET OF DEATH and achieved to control it. What makes a god "god" is the fact that he has the knowledge of the secrets of the power of all the relevant potentialities that have been evoked since the first sound in the universe. The Gods cannot create the will of the universe. The first sound is the real parent of humans. That is why the human soul is a music that begins with sound and comes into being through a transformation. You will read in this book the journey of the soul that becomes ready to incarnate once transformed into music.

The book is a textbook as well. It especially possesses gifts to offer to those astrologers who aim to specialize in reincarnation in astrology. It is a book full of interesting information, methods and perspectives which I hope will inspire you. I wish that it will support you in your journey of making life more meaningful and peaceful for you, your families and your clients…

Are you ready to take the journey to the End of the Earth and to here, from the Threshold of that End? Are you ready for death and life?

**Let us begin then.**

*Ahura Sevgi Alis Yıldırım*

# CHAPTER I

Let us leave behind the memorized definitions of reincarnation and go back to its essential theses so that we can fully grasp what it really is. Here are the essential theses of reincarnation:

*1. There is a soul and a body, and they are two separate beings.*

*2. The soul has all the knowledge. In its DNA storage, the body keeps the memory of other humans who lived on Earth before us, i.e., our ancestors. And it transmits that memory from one generation to another.*

*3. Learning is actually remembering. (In honor of Plato's famous saying: "knowing is remembering")*

*4. Everything that exists is constantly in transformation. Everything in nature is in interaction with one another and continue their transformation every moment by affecting one another.*

We experience duality on this planet, which creates a very interesting story. We exist in accordance with the flow, the principles and natural laws of this planet. We are a final result that is derived after "a series of awakenings" as a result of the interaction between the evoked potentials. Therefore, ***as beings who produce thoughts, we are the purpose of the universe. We are the result of the evoked potentials. We are awakened potentials.*** Being human was just one of our potentials. The main purpose of the universe for itself is to construct a system that can produce thoughts. Being able to start thinking is the vital source of energy production that is necessary for the universe to continue its existence and incarnation. In a way, ***man is the nutritional source of the universe.*** Man is very precious. The forces who know this great secret have always forbidden men to kill one another, and man is just learning to give up this bad practice because deep down, he feels the impossibility of dying.

What is a human? Human is a potential in the universe. Whatever this potential interacts with, it becomes a subject to the principles of this new space and takes shape according to them. This relationship is definitely mutual. This potential transmits all the other potentials that are in accordance with those principles into the memory of the planet as well. The human is potentially a "memory". ***He is not an ordinary transmitter. He is the memory itself. The human is the memory of the universe.***

He carries the knowledge of being the memory of the universe in his DNA and his spiritual transformation. The human consists of bodies, which indicates that he transmits knowledge from each level of his bodies. ***The human is the awakened potential. The human is time. He is a "knowledge"***

***awakened in the memory of the universe.*** This knowledge, that is the human, is activated when a light becomes sufficient in its evolution towards being a soul, interacts with the planet Earth and takes a place in the field of duality. Therefore, it is not the human who brings duality onto his planet. Because the human has not come to this planet from another place. What comes to this planet is the "sound" that has become sufficient (music). ***The human is born out of the unification of the heavenly soul and the earthly body.*** Therefore it is not possible for a person to be 'from another planet'. So, "I am a Martian" is not a correct statement. No, as a human, you can't be a Martian. You can only transform into a human on Earth.

Your soul, which is the part of you that makes you human here, might have hit the light of Mars, "brewed" in its aura and incarnated there untill it reached the maturity to be attracted towards the activity field of Earth. This doesn't make you a Martian. Mars is the place where your soul has prepared for incarnation; so that it could form the human by unifying with a body. The two expressions are very different. A human is only human on Earth. You can neither state "I consist of only spirit", nor can you say "I am only my body." Your body is from Earth and yes, your soul definetly comes from a planet.

A potential, whether spirit or body, is obliged to enter into the field of duality in order to become *humanized*. The physical body originates on Earth while the soul originates in the "primordial sound" (the sky). You know that, as being a law of Earth, the main function of duality is to create time; in other words, to make the Earth's potential become visible. Duality expresses itself in the completion of water-earth and that of air-fire. This is the first law. The Earth is already a potential and a memory. In this regard, the Earth itself is a time corridor in its own right. The Earth has has gained this state by staying in a sufficient level of interaction with the other potentials in the universe. We exist on a planet that has achieved to reach one of the most privileged and special levels that a planet can ever reach in this universe. As a living being, The Earth loves to attract us, the dear souls, towards itself. It loves to host us, be in relationship with us and attract us into the field of her own laws. It wants it. It desires it.

As long as our souls exist in this field; the Earth, thus the universe as well, can attain a very special level in their own incarnation process. The Earth, and the universe, need us in their own process of incarnation. The universe needs a centre. And this centre is not single. There are always certain centres for a certain field. For instance, Sun and Earth are two centres whose functions we are aware of. If we accept Sun to be the centre of the universe, we acknowledge that the first light which was evoked by the primordial sound as the reference for the centre of all manifestation.

Taking Sun as the centre of the universe will finally take us to music, which is the soul, and the reference for the initial manifestation of human will be "music" (soul). However, if we take the Earth as the centre of the universe, we will realize that matter manifests itself from itself, regard Earth as the beating heart of the universe and understand that the first reference point in the process of human's manifestation is matter. Who can ever claim that neither of them are correct? Both are correct depending on your perspective. Nevertheless, the essential truth is the possibility that both can be correct at the same time. This might sound as a logical error at first; yet what makes it not so is the fact that we create a thought in a certain space and from a certain direction in the universe. What makes us think as the reference point of manifestation is nothing but the place you are at and its direction.

The system of the Earth's incarnation process is based on duality. So why is there duality on our Earth? Why does the universe experience it? If we take the fact "the universe's ultimate aim is creating thoughts" as a premise, it would be quite understandable to think of duality as a unique tool that serves this aim. Because ***the universe wants to think itself.*** It produces more energy and much more effective energies as it thinks of itself. We can consider this as a fuel, a nourishment. ***The universe becomes more creative as we continue to think.*** This must be completely related to the reincarnation of the universe.

If we closely examine duality; we will see that it is the circumstance that caused the Earth to attain its current state aeons ago, when we did not exist here. An Earth that exists through duality needs us, the human incarnations in order to maintain its existence. We help Mother Earth and the whole universe through our manifestation. Let me clarify this point: We are not here to help the animals, water or plants. This is not true. Our connection with these beings are not based on our actions of protecting and saving them or taking care of them. They do not need such an assistance anyway.

The life on the Earth's incarnation have flourished based on the 4 elements because it could evoke the water-earth, air-fire duality from its potential. The water-earth has become a reference point of duality in itself. And air-fire has become a reference point of duality in itself too. The relationship between the two brings forth knowledge, which unites with other types of knowledge. This continues forever. This reference point of duality has, after all, begun to incarnate the activated potentials in accordance with the laws. We call the awakened potential "animal". We call the other awakened potentials "plants". And we call another potential that was awakened, "human". Each potential is evoked in the field that it interacts with. The souls of us, the humans, experiences itself as a body here, when it gets into interaction with this planet. Who could ever know how our awakened potential seems when it is in interaction with another planet? Or can it ever be seen at all? Who knows how this potential seem like each time it is awakened… As you know, whatever it is that awakens us, we begin to manifest according to its laws.

The planets need souls like us when the right time comes for them to incarnate. We are not beings that the Earth has given birth to by itself. It is true that only our bodies come from the Earth. The meteors that frequently fall from the sky etc, get mixed into our Earth's water, earth or air. After all these meteor decompositions transform into parts of the Earth. So we can state that our bodies are completely from Earth. In other words, we are not orphan bodies that were left here. We are beings that have been shaped and awakened by interacting with the Earth and becoming a part of Earth's circle of duality and going through a filter. That is all.

So where do our souls come from? The answer is: Nowhere. The souls do not go on a tour in the galaxy choosing planetary resorts for themselves. The light goes through certain stages in order to become a soul in the galaxy. The last stage is being a soul. So when the light reaches that maturity, it sets off towards Earth's aura, joins the movement and begins to incarnate in duality. So this light has no desire other than reaching the Earth since the moment it has become a soul. Therefore, instead of saying "our souls come from this or that place", I prefer to express 'My light has transformed into a soul on this planet, 'steeped' there and then was attracted into the *turbulance* of the Earth. If I said "My soul has come from Mars", that would mean that I had been living on Mars and then moved to this planet, which would be a misunderstanding.

These potentials are sufficient for something to be in interaction or awaken. We are eternal potentials that have awakened. Most philosophers in history tried to grasp this truth. It is natural for an awakened potential to seek itself. Philosophers are the seekers of our species. Seizing the "moment"!...Seizing "the moment" is their main task. They are conscious that everything they see and interact with is a web of a potential in itself. What I learnt from the philosophers on a mental level was their effort to comprehend duality by understanding it. They later appealed to the concept of explaining in order to improve and expand their understanding. And they chose to explain things following their quest so that they can express new things. This is called positive science. A journey from science of antiquity to positive science… Mere explanation signifies an avoidance of the responsibility of knowledge. See, if we try to explain things through experimenting and observation, that means we carefully abstain from taking the responsibility of nature's actions. I suggest that instead of asking "Should I comprehend by understanding, or explaining?", we can choose to take the responsibility of both explaining and understanding……. That means we totally take the responsibility of the state of "knowing" to the full extent. *Learning is remembering*, yes! Remembering requires a complete devotion which had led those like Bruno to be burned.

It has led us to heavy taxation, hurting the people, unjust distribution of the sources, expansion of the wars and increase in population. A state of knowing without a responsibility will eventually accuse the World and makes one say: "This is the way the World is, what can I do?" This will lead us and the World to a next phase, which means new levels of interactions. That is why some companies out there search for livable planets in behalf of our species. We should understand that the reason of the unpleasant events we experience when the knowledge of Earth's manifestation is used for malignant purposes. The choice of "explaining" which made us abstain from the responsibility of knowing, led us to leave behind our interaction with the World and search for new interactions in new planets. Meanwhile, the Earth continues to experience its duality. It wouldn't wait for us. Fundamentally, it doesn't live for us. *We* live for the whole universe.

This is what all the philosophers did: comprehending duality. By this way, they would know, to what and for what reason we, as a potential, are awakening. So they would be able to discover physical immortality as well. Keep it in your mind: there is fear of death at the heart of any progress in human life. We cannot recall the idea of death every moment because deep down the humans know that they are not mortal spiritually. Yet we cannot stand the idea of a physical death and we are even trying to overcome infinity. The common question of all the philosophers is "What can we do so that our bodies will not die?", is it not? The philosophers thought. The thoughts met the matter and transferred into our lives through systems of faith. Then it dawned on us that all those thoughts extended the life span of our species in every generation. This is the greatest proof. All the sciences in the world, without any exception, function together. What comes out as an output is in accordance with the nature of Hermeticism. That is to say; our life span is expanding. Don't you realize that everybody is talking about freedom, regeneration, rebirth and saying "We are immortal!" nowadays? A new faith is being born. These indicate nothing but an effort to activate a new potential and create new corridors of time by transforming the memory circle of the world by using the human consciousness. This is an effort of overcoming the duality. The whole history of thought seems to serve this purpose.

Make a list of all the inspiring philosophers in history and study the knowledge they achieved to grasp and interpret. You will see a common fundamental point in all of them without any exception; they are all wise people who have a distinct capability to unite the opposites in a fascinating way. They came up with their most brilliant ideas only when they made up their mind to unite opposite poles. And when they did achieve to unite the opposites, they used the energy created by this unification. Each one of these thinkers helped some two forces, which were seemingly opposite and different, come into a direct contact with another.

The concept of contact is crucial. Because this is how the new, undiscovered corridors of time, which can be compared to a library that have empty shelves, come into existence. Time can be built easily through the contact of two opposite poles.

This must have created an amazing insight and a profound feeling of content with regards to understanding life and the end of it. I believe the idea of overcoming duality and the feeling of having a control on duality creates the most satisfactory state for our species. The desire of overcoming duality is a wonderful expectation and invention. Whenever we bring the two opposites together in order to overcome duality, they definitely unite. And this new knowledge immediately produces its opposite. That's how the life can proceed. New corridors of time are built and "the nourishment of knowledge" increases.

*Because life is only possible with time (memory).*

Being able to understand duality inspires us to release the concept of "immortality" from only being a feeling or aspiration. It inspires us to transform immortality into a comprehendible, applicable form. It is the demystified duality principle that builds and organizes 'the dying' of a body. It is a perfect reference point for the immortality of a body. This is the victory of the Earth. It means that the humans fulfill their function for the Earth in the most complete and perfect way.

2. The Earth yearns for interacting with our souls. It needs us for its own incarnation. Do we not need it too? This is definitely a mutual relation; yet this is not the main subject of my book. I will be tackling this issue in another book. **The main purpose of Remember is to contribute to the understanding that death is impossible.**

*Reincarnation is a mechanism the Earth uses to overcome duality, which basically means continuously uniting the opposite poles thus activating and accelerating the birth of new opposite poles.* We incarnate for the universe. We are awakened potentials that manifested in physical from on this Earth. *We are a song that the Universe is humming.* We are all perfect beings with equal worth and value. We are special beings of a high frequency. We are very valuable. We are souls that are so much desired and have such intense potentials that came to a planet because it needed us.

Awaken to who you are. **Remember who you are!** It will not dawn on you all of a sudden. It will awaken in you only through a realization that will take over each particle in your physical body and a deep feeling of satisfaction. It is not like an apple you can reach and pick from the branch of a tree. It is just there, waiting to be awakened. Something either sleeps or awakens in the universe. That is all! It is nature's unique function to awaken a potential. That is why they attempt to use the way of 'explaining' instead of comprehending, in order to understand this behavior of nature, which is a way to avoid the possible destructive responsibility on masses. Such a way of "explaining" expresses itself as the science of psychology.

The relationship between the one that stimulates and the one that is awakened is the basis of this science. I am sure your realize that Plato's interesting formula which survived for thousands of years cost humanity a great price: 'knowing is remembering'. The meaning of this formula is so powerful; it summarizes the consciousness of existing, which has been structured for centuries, in a very simple and understandable way. Nevertheless, we can see this fascinating genius, years later being an inspiration of the Jewish holocaust. What Plato remembers is found in his "Republic" which inspired Hitler and triggered a non-ecological force. Therefore, ***we should be very careful about what we are awakening to and what it is that we are remembering.*** It might cause a destruction.

Humanity has learnt and is still learning it through painful experiences. ***What one remembers might bring a disaster for another.*** The Earth cannot benefit in any way from our deliberate actions of destroying one another. This deliberate destruction is a part of the potential of the "human phenomenon".

Man's impulse to destroy arises from the need of the living beings to eat when hungry and to create and preserve resources to feel safe. The need for security in animals, plants or other living beings are completely different than that of humans. They even do not have a need for security in terms of what the humans do. The humans might have taken on such a quality because of being exposed to duality; yet this doesn't mean that their potential is not active in other time-space levels.

I feel that there is a connection between our current state and our existence in other time and space dimensions. And we continuously transfer "memory" to one another via this connection. Let us imagine the following now so that we can express it easily. Imagine that you have Mars on your right, Venus on your left, Earth on the north and Saturn on the south. Visualize a ball of intense light that continuously spins in itself at the center of these four planets. Let us call this ball of light "potential". These spheres have a precession in themselves, and they can rotate around their axis with a ceaseless rhythm and tempo as they create their music. That is to say, they create sound since they can move.

Through this sound, they can designate their energetic field (their aura). The sounds they make mix with one another. These sounds can transfer the convenient information through the proper tunnel of time with the help of factors such as the speed and direction of the movement in the existent tunnel of time. This point should be understood very well.

By this way it will be possible to understand the qualities of the distribution of memory as well as how, where, why and when the energy (memory, information) that is required for the incarnation will be used. That is why the "remembering time" of each planet should be known well. By this way, we will understand how the universe incarnates itself very well, which signifies a network for transferring information. You will see how the energy required for the incarnation flows in the corridors of time in a perfect way. The incarnation process continues to proceed whether we are aware of it.

***Remembering is "awakening".*** The manifestation of the time required for the reincarnation becomes easier since the flow of information leads to the manifestation of new information, which is the awakening of potentials. The whole process of remembering is to increase the manifestation of time. Because ***the setting (environment) for karma is "time"***. In this way, everything will continue to exist every moment. ***Remembering is "reincarnating". Remembering is the awakening of knowledge and formation of time.*** Now I will teach you what I mean by this concept of "remembering". I will reveal the knowledge step by step. And I am writing this book exactly for this purpose.

*"Remembering is Reincarnating."*

**Remember**

# TIMES OF REMEMBERING

If I explain the most effective times for remembering, I will help you to recognize the period knowledge awakens and to control your process of remembering. Thus, you will have the opportunity to create your own time.

I will teach a few methods to do that, first of which is following the Moon phases.

## Remembering According to Moon phases:

Moon phases last 28 days on average. So why does the Moon do that? Why does this intelligence have such a relationship with Earth and other celestial elements? Let me answer it with a story which I hope you will enjoy. Let us dream. The Moon is a karma-neutralizing tool. This is a strange sentence, isn't it? I know that it is, but I can only start with such a sentence to explain what I have in my mind. Do not worry, it will all be clear as you read the book.

The greatest function of Moon might be hidden in its act of taking the energy (memory) that Earth is emitting from its aura and bringing it to the End of the Earth (center of the Earth or the field of gravity), which is the 'Land of the Dead'. Think of it this way; by continuously rotating around our planet, Moon records in its aura all the energy that we emit into the universe. The Moon has chakras too and these information are attracted into its related chakras. Moon has 8 chakras, which are phases.

## Phases of the Moon:

1- New Moon: 0-44 degrees; Aries. The dispositor of this chakra is Mars.

2- Crescent: 45-89 degrees; Taurus and Gemini. The dispositors of this chakra are Venus and Mercury. Because this chakra has two stages.

3- First quarter: 90-134 degrees; Cancer and Leo. The dispositors of this chakra are Moon and Sun. Because this chakra has two stages.

4- Waxing Moon: 135-179 degrees; Virgo. The dispositor of this chakra is Mercury.

5- Full Moon: 180-224 degrees; Libra. The dispositor of this chakra is Venus.

6- Waning Moon: 225-269 degrees; Scorpio and Sagittarius. The dispositors of this chakra are Pluto and Jupiter. Because this chakra has two stages.

7- Last Quarter Moon: 270-314 degrees; Capricorn-Aquarius. The dispositor of this chakra are Saturn and Uranus. Because this chakra has two stages.

8-. Balsamic Moon: 315-360 degrees; Pisces. The dispositor of this chakra is Neptune.

Each time, one of the chakras of the Moon is on the agenda depending on its motion. We call the chakra activation 'a phase of the Moon'. You know that the activation of the chakras of the Moon is a result of its relation with the Sun in terms of distance. Because it is only the Sunlight that can activate Moon's chakras. Earth or any other planet does not have the activation of Moon's chakras in their agenda. This is the natural plan.

**The 1$^{st}$ phase is always the New Moon.**
When Moon conjunct Sun at the same degree and minute, a fully bright and new energy, i.e. a brand new time frame, begins to be constructed. The 1$^{st}$ chakra of the Moon is activated at this phase. This chakra has the nature of Mars. The field which is constructed by the karmic information emerges from such a state. This is also where the karmic information will be collected. In short, the memory of karma initially begins to build its own time in this field. Mars initiates this primary time frame. This section of time is a brand new energy, it is just a "beginner" yet. It is open to direction and

guidance. It doesn't have a past. Because it is just being created.

### The 2nd phase is always Crescent.

In this chakra, the Moon records the memory which transformed into matter from the energy we had created on Earth for 3.6 days. It receives the karmic memory of matter into this chakra through the influence of the lights of Venus and Mercury. This second frame of time is constructed by Venus and Mercury so this is the first chakra in which the energy of matter and human are recorded. The energies of matter and human get recorded here to be later transferred to the *End of the Earth*.

### The 3rd phase is always the First Quarter.

Throughout the 3.6 days, the Moon records in this chakra its (Moon's) own function that reflects on Earth and the memory that is created through the power of thought. Here, the light that reflects from the Moon onto the Earth transforms into emotion and returns back to Moon as memory. The function of the Moonlight as a uniting force should be understood well. What holds us together is a gift of the Moonlight that reflects to us. It is our emotion. Moon is our personal memory and our own end (heart), which is our center. It is the part of us that connects us to death. It is our heart chakra. ***Moon is the heart chakra of the***

***human***. The Sun keeps us alive and Moon is the greatest power that holds us together. And all this memory settles in the 3$^{rd}$ chakra of the Moon.

**The 4$^{th}$ phase is always the Waxing Moon.** Throughout these 3,6 days, Moon records in this chakra the memory of what we, humans, do for others. *What did you do for others?* Mercury rules this chakra since it is Mercury that meticulously weaves the memory here. Mercury asks us: *"What did you do for your physical body?"*. It transfers the memory related to the protection of the physical body. This is the first chakra in which the information about physical human body gets recorded. The specific themes are starting, creating matter, thoughts, emotions and finally the physical human body, sensitivity and caring for others. All these information get recorded in the 4$^{th}$ chakra.

**The 5$^{th}$ phase is always Full Moon.**

Moon records in its 4$^{th}$ chakra humans' actions to start something, to transform the energy of the former four phases into matter, to reach knowledge, their progress, the power of their emotions and thoughts as well as what they do for one another and for their own physical bodies. In its Full Moon phase, the Moon encourages us to let go of the karma we created. It asks us: *"Can you now let go of the matter you created as well as your thoughts, your emotions and everything you are attached to?"* Here, we are in the presence of a Moonlight that has the mission of teaching us not to be a prisoner of what we create.

In this phase, the Moon initiates the test of attachment, in other words, the test of overcoming the matter. And we go through a test where we learn not to be a prisoner of what we manifest. ***We are forced to learn how to let go.*** That is why Venus is the energy that takes the first step here in order to awaken the highest consciousness. Venus in this phase confronts Mars (Aries) and takes on its first recognized mission amongst all the signs, which is being a MIRROR.

***Full Moon is the phase where all the memory accumulated under the Moonlight (the first 4 chakras) is reflected back to Earth.*** And it is the most interesting phase. Through this chakra, Venus holds a mirror to humanity for 3.6 days each month to test how much we can improve our consciousness level. ***This is the phase where the Moon, being our mother, begins to give its first "motherly upbringing and discipline".*** And her first lesson is the following: *"Whatever it may be that you manifest, do not be a prisoner of the matter or other people, do not be a prisoner of your labor, thoughts or emotions! Because it is your duty to overcome the matter so that you can* *proceed. You manifested the matter in order to overcome it."*

**The 6th phase is always Waning Moon.**
In this chakra, the Moon continues to discipline and educate us for something spectacular during the 3.6 days. There is the purpose of teaching two kinds of great knowledge in this phase of the *Moon school*, first of which is dominated by Pluto. The reason behind the Full Moon's teaching of letting go everything we create and are attached to is revealed in this very phase. *Because Pluto signifies the most distinct point of overcoming the matter. A human's target in his evolution is always going to the End of the Earth. Because humans, due to the nature of their mission on this Earth, desire experiencing the descent to the center of the Earth so as to be able to rise again to the surface.* A soul that passes Pluto's test can achieve it on Earth.

Here is what this phase is teaching us: *'You can produce the matter. And your purpose of producing matter is to learn to go beyond it. There is eternity beyond that, which is being out of time. This is the phase of "experiencing death while still living". This phase targets to teach the privilege of going into the utmost depth and beyond time. Our focus is no longer on the physical body; it deepens towards the body's source. When our focus moves away from the physical body, it also partially drifts away from thoughts and feelings, and thus physical ailments heal easily as well.'*

Pluto is the physician here. Jupiter has a wonderful role in this phase. Human race experiences *death* and how to stay connected to higher realms while living. Jupiter's duty is to make this "obscurity" clear and distinct for humans. Jupiter does that by "transforming the wisdom of emptiness into a relevant belief and form". Jupiter weaves its light in humans so that they can turn the wisdom they derive from contacting the emptiness in themselves, into belief. The energy that is transferred into the aura of a person who is exposed to the wisdom in the field of Pluto, which is the wisdom of the beyond, manifests itself as *belief* on this planet. What turns that energy into belief is the light of Jupiter.

### The 7$^{th}$ phase is the Last Quarter.

During the 3.6 days in this chakra, Moon focuses on the story of humans who create matter and achieve to overcome it. As you notice, Moon exposes humans to the two poles of duality during the time of its first 6 chakras. So, the Moon first teaches humans how to create matter and energies close to matter; and then how to let go of it. In this way, it teaches how to go beyond matter, in other words, beyond life.

**It teaches humans, who are now "back from death's door" and incarnated, to structure time 'as a belief' in a mature way.**

It teaches humans, who are now "back from death's door" and reincarnated, to structure time in a mature way. *Finally, Saturn gets involved to create the information of the year until which a person, who has experienced life with its polarity, will continue to live. In other words, the life span is specified. This cycle repeats itself, again and again, each month.* Saturn records in its aura all the memories that emerge out of experiencing the two poles of life, as the original memory of karma. Saturn always does that through the Moon. It especially attracts the karmic information in nature in the Last Quarter phase. Uranus takes the information that reaches Saturn's memory via Moon's $7^{th}$ chakra and transfers this information into different areas as a "nourishment". This book actually leads me to write another book so that I can explain this subject.

**The 8th phase is always Last Quarter.**

For 3.6 days, this chakra of the Moon is about transforming all that karmic memory created by a person who has been exposed to the secrets of duality into inspiration. Here we meet Neptune that transfers the karmic memory to the end of the universe. To put it romantically, we humans turn into an inspiration under the light of Neptune, with the help of the energy we created in the test of life throughout the lights of these phases. Maybe *it was never Neptune that inspired*. Maybe *inspiration is nothing but the reflection of our transformed karmic energy that had been received by Neptune's memory.* Maybe *inspiration is nothing other than ourselves.*

So, why do the Moon phases exist?

The planets can fully function under the moonlight. When the Moon reflects its light on Earth, the light of the other planets easily becomes functional and powerful on Earth. The Moon also is a guarantee, a vehicle, for the light of the planets to function on Earth. Its function is incredibly powerful. This is Moon's essential mission for us. Everything, day and night, take place in the Moonlight. In the *school of Moon*, we are regularly subject to a cycle every day, phase and month. Here is how the cycle works: We first begin to do something new, then our effort becomes matter. And we create emotions, thoughts, labor etc. Then we are attached to matter and our own *productions*. At the Full Moon, we are challenged to let go of the matter, and energies close to matter, that we create. This is the test of the Earth and matter. It is one of the poles of duality. ***We are suddenly led to emptiness with a great depth once our attachment to matter ceases to stand in our way. And it encourages us to experience death while still living.*** What is mentioned here is definitely not the death of a physical body. This is a spiritual intention. The emptiness reveals itself to us as "belief". And we finally connect the End of the Earth to here (where we are now). As we experience matter and what's beyond matter in a systematic way (whether consciously or not), we produce the karmic memory, i.e. the information or time, that is powerful enough to settle in Saturn's memory.

I wonder if Uranus is happy to find new "sounds" in the connection between universes? Or is Neptune happy to have a new memory that serves the emptiness of the universe? I will write in another book what Neptune does with that memory. Take note that we witness how the karmic energy we create is carried in the whole universe, as well as other universes, beyond Saturn, which represents the ultimate point where the knowledge of an Earthly incarnation can reach.

Let us study what the planets represent closely. Could what we call "the essence of the planets" be a "back reflection" of the energy that emerges out of our experience of the two poles of duality in the light of the phases? Our knowledge is transformed and evolved after they are embedded in the aura of the planets. Could they be just 'molding' what they take from us in their own image and reflecting it back to us? Could it be that what reflects from them is nothing but our own light and karmic memory? My answer is YES. When you trace the Moon phases, you easily understand that what it is that reflects back to you and supports you. And you can act accordingly. Moon's $8^{th}$ phase is the Balsamic phase. It is the end of the time that is manifested specially for that particular month in terms of karma. Time is *dead* for approximately 3.5 days after the Balsamic phase.

That's why **nothing that we start at the New Moon phase, when the Moon's light is not present in the sky, "flourishes"**. It can't proceed to become materialized. Because the **Moon Mother is having her appointment with the mystery of death and the essential light that helps us to create time is not present in the sky. You cannot create karma when the Moon is not in the sky. You can't build time.** You know that. The seed you plant won't sprout, what you sow will not yield. There have been generations that saw what they pickled or prepared at this particular time was spoiled and went sour. Our efforts to create matter is only possible through the Moon's light. We experience uncertainty for almost 3.5 days when it is not present in the sky.

Yes, that's our story.

The energy of the Moon's chakras reflects in our duality-based Earth and our lives by being transformed into such qualities. After recording in its chakras the energy of the karma we create, the Moon goes to the *End of the Earth* to discharge this memory. And it transfers all the memory into a central point where motion *stops*. In order to do that, the Moon needs to unite with the Sunlight.

At the New Moon phase, there is a renewed, refreshed, and relieved Moon that had discharged the memory in its chakras, running towards the Crescent phase (the matter). During these approximately 3.5 days, "the beginning of time" is being formed once again. This sacred light collects all the karmic memory that is produced until the end of the 28 day- period. And it repeatedly goes to the *End of the Earth* to discharge its memory. This cycle is extremely meaningful in its own right.

## The Skill of Using Retrograde Periods of Planets to Remember Past Lives:

Both lights and planets are beings that incarnate. Every object that moves was exposed to the strike of 'the first sound'. It began to move, at the moment of the strike, which basically means that it transformed from being an *infinite potential* into an *awakened potential*. It then began to construct its own time. Any potential that awakens, i.e. begins to move, after being exposed to "sound", inevitably begins to make sound. Through this sound, it hits infinite numbers of potentials around and awakens them, which sets them in motion too. This causes the emergence of "new sounds". It is like a chain interaction. A little movement in one makes all the other potentials around move. Each object interacts with the others in its surrounding, making them vibrate and awakening their potential. They are exposed to the same process by others. These vibrations mutually awaken potentials, after which interesting shapes, concrete objects, myriad of things that we call new and finally "music" emerge. Any potential that has such an activity has to incarnate. Otherwise, it can't move on.

The Moon does not go retrograde. Nevertheless, the Moon doesn't show its light in the sky for almost 3.5 days. This is a process that we can perceive as a retrograde. Science explains it clearly. On the other hand, we, the spiritual researchers express the scientific explanation using our own language and approach. Using the astrological language, we can state that for 28 days, the Moon directs its focus to the *Centre of the Earth* in order to discharge our karmic memory that it had accumulated in its chakras during the phases it reflected its light to us. It can be regarded as a "retrograde motion of the Moon". It also means that the retrograde of the planets discharge the karmic memory accumulated in their chakras into the relevant spaces. The planets need that activation.

*The Centre of the Earth* is one of the "Centers" where the planets and Moon discharge the karmic memory. They bring all our data back into our "Centre", which is our reference point. They bring back whatever was done. That is why the essential thesis of Hermeticism is; "as above, so below."

A memory (Moon and planets) reflects our karmic memory, which expands from the Earth into the universe, back to us... We should understand this process very well. In retrograde periods, the habit of creating karma according to a rhythm (tempo) familiar to Nature is replaced by a different one, which generally results in a sense of slowing down in time. We call it delay, postponement or hindrance. Nevertheless, neither of them is in question.

What's in question is the temporary change in the pace of the energy that flows between the Earth and the planets & Moon. Because the planets begin to discharge (transfer) our karmic information, accumulated in their chakras, into our "Centre". When this information transfer is over, they once again go back to their former rhythm and we perceive them as "having turned direct". When in reality, it is our sphere that got faster.

Through our mobility, we give them a chance to transfer us the information. They never go back or stop. We are the ones that go fast. They once again collect our karmic information in their chakras and wait for the right time to discharge the memory. While the planets and the Moon discharge all the accumulated memories into the *Centre of the Earth* (field of gravity), you can benefit from this extraordinary process by attracting the information of your past memories into your body.

It becomes easier to remember since the "books of the past" are revealed over and over as the information is flowing into our 'Centre'. The foremost thing you should do in order to attract the information of the past memories into your body (which means awakening the knowledge in your chakras) is being in harmony with the rhythm of the retrograde, which is keeping up with the rhythm of the retrograde motion.

What kind of a knowledge and method would easily help you to awaken the memories in your chakras? The answer is that you must do the relevant meditation. I will suggest you two different ways which are explained in the following. You do not have to choose one, you may practice both.

**1. Shortened remembering exercise based on phases:** I suggest you a practical approach for this one. Let us assume that you want to attract information at the New Moon phase, which means awakening knowledge in your chakra. New Moon lasts for about 3.5 days. It consists of seven 12 hours, which makes 84 hours. You can awaken the knowledge for yourself by doing an 84-minute meditation (seven times 12 minutes) every day during these 3.5 days.

**2. Remembering exercise based on the retrograde motion of a planet:** Here is another helpful exercise you can practice. Let's suppose that Mercury is retrograde for 20 days. I suggest that you meditate for 1440 minutes. If you meditate for 72 minutes every day (six times 12 minutes), it will make 1440 minutes in 20 days (twenty times 72 minutes). And it will be easy for you to awaken the knowledge that is crucial for you.

The purpose of this method is to align time by fully activating the *seventy-twos* in 12 houses, 12 signs and the relevant hemisphere in the 360 degree-cycle of the Zodiac. The target is opening the door of the 72°. Starting from the ASC as the reference point, the two consecutive 72 degrees take us to a point 6 degrees before the 6$^{th}$ house. We slow down 6 degrees before the gate of the 6$^{th}$ sign. There remains 36 degrees until the end of the Northern hemisphere. Here, the only way to open the "Gate of Mercury" is awakening two high skills. Check the exact points of the first and second 72nd degree. These two degrees are the points through which your special talents can easily be activated. Therefore, two significant talents you had in your past life can be awakened to support you in your current life.

This is how we approach the planets in this chapter of the book.

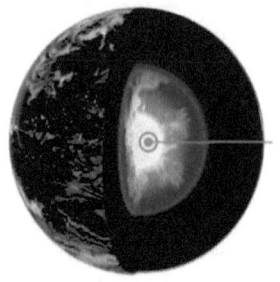

The Heart of the Earth

## The Retrograde and Remembering:

Each planet and Moon have karmic memories. Retrograde periods need to be followed in order to discover the memories. All the planets, without any exception, record in their auras and chakras, the memory of the karma of a specific area in the world. In the retrograde period, they transfer these records to the *End of the Earth* (the gravity, or heart, of the Earth). In this way, the memory reaches the reference point of the Earth, which is the *End of the Earth*. There is an activation each time this memory reaches the reference point of the Earth. For instance, Mars records the karmic memory of all the dynamism; wars, accidents, ambitions etc. in its chakras for months. And when it begins its retrograde motion, Mars activates a time corridor between the Earth and itself. This is a type of a channel. Imagine that there is a cord between our Earth and the planets & the Moon, just like the umbilical cord between a mother and a baby. What are activated are these time tunnels.

***These time corridors are activated to transfer information. And we call the general situation that arises throughout the process of the functioning of the activated channel as "the retrograde".*** When the process of discharging memories is completed, the time corridor "falls asleep" once again. And we say, "the planet completed its retrograde motion." ***However, as you notice, the retrograde is a process of transferring information.*** Think of it as a gate that slightly opens its doors. ***What actually takes place during this process is the story of the opening of the gates of the karma.***

The retrograde periods are fairly liberated and unique times. Knowing that there is a dance in the sky towards Pluto and the karmic memory is transferring itself in the form of "the retrograde", we should keep up with this rhythm and act in the direction of the retrograde motion. Let us turn into the retrograde rhythm itself, instead of resisting the flow of nature that we perceive as a slowing down during those days. Let us keep step with the rhythm of the time corridors that are activated. Let us learn to dance with the rhythm of the knowledge that is being transferred so that our memories can awaken easily in our chakras. Let us hear the "music of our spheres", the lights that transform into souls by steeping in the auras of the planets.

**The end of the human is his heart chakra.** The Earth also has an end, namely a heart chakra. All the karmic memory flows into the heart chakra and our heart chakra is directly connected to the Earth's heart chakra. Therefore, during the retrograde periods, we can easily remember the knowledge that flows into the Earth's heart by using a relevant method. The most useful one is definitely meditation. I can teach you how you should meditate. All you need is a whole-hearted intention.

The list is as follows:

- *Meditate to remember the memory of Venus when Venus begins its retrograde motion.*
- *Meditate to remember the memory of Mars when Mars begins its retrograde motion.*
- *Meditate to remember the memory of Mercury when Mercury begins its retrograde motion.*
- *Meditate to remember the memory of Jupiter when Jupiter begins its retrograde motion.*

**Remembering Saturn's memory, whether it's Saturn's retrograde period or not, means remembering the memory of all your lives.** Different than the other planets, Saturn already comprises the memories of all the other planets in its aura. ***Opening Saturn's memory means revealing the knowledge of all chakras.*** If that is true, why do we need to practice separately for the memory of each single planet?

If Saturn records all the knowledge, we should only be interested in opening Saturn's aura. Wouldn't that be easier? Yes, that is a good question. My answer is; once your karmic information settles in the memory of a planet, it unites with the planet's energy and incarnates there. ***In order to have a direct connection with your parts that get incarnated on other planets, you need to practice planetary exercises.*** Because Saturn does not know what your karmic information has transformed into on these planets. ***It doesn't know about the process of the formation of a soul that will incarnate.*** Therefore, Saturn can't know about the information a soul may have received from other planets before incarnating. After it enters a body, your soul continues to transmit to the planets the information of the karma you create on Earth. Who knows, what type of a karmic information you are transferring to a chakra of Venus right now and what you are transforming into on that planet. Saturn can't know this. ***Saturn only dominates and stores your memories on Earth.*** Uranus, Pluto, and Neptune retrogrades represent completely different meanings. Therefore, they are not included in this list.

Each of the mentioned meditations have the Moon in their focal point. The first thing you need to do for initiating the remembering process is always remembering tranquility. Otherwise the system will not work for you. ***Remembering tranquility is being initiated into what you perceive as "emptiness".*** Initiation into emptiness is the most essential exercise. This might not be easy to comprehend at first. But please relax, I will teach it in the simplest way. I know that there are much intriguing exercises for that purpose in the times of antiquity, but what I teach you is the easiest and most enjoyable one. I will present you an exercise which the philosopher Alexander Imsiragic has taught me, who has also been a consultant in my process of writing this book. Here is how I first learnt to be initiated into emptiness.

### *Exercise for Initiation into Emptiness:*

Sit in an upright position in a silent place and close your eyes. ***You need to close your eyes to the world outside in order to open them into your inner world.*** Relax your body to its smallest particles by doing a breathing exercise. This might take several minutes, there is no particular limit as to how much it should take; it is up to the meditator. When you are totally relaxed, feel the couch or chair you are sitting on and feel that you become one with it.

Continue until you completely feel and sense that the couch/ chair and your body are one and the same thing. Then focus on the center of the room and feel the emptiness in the room. Continue to relax and feel that you are one with all the furniture in the room, the door, the windows and the walls. Feel that they are parts of your body. You will then feel that the emptiness gets deeper and deeper as you remain in that state for a while. The feeling of emptiness can only be experienced, it can't be expressed.

It is very usual not to have the result you might have expected the first time your try it. Because this initiation should be repeated at least for 20 minutes every day for 28 days. It doesn't have to be at the same hour each day, but make sure you do it at least once a day. You shouldn't start this 28 day-exercise, "initiation into emptiness", at the New Moon phase when you don't see the Moon's light in the sky. You may choose any other phase of the Moon. If you forget to repeat the exercise for one day, you should start the 28-day cycle counting from *day 1* in the following day.

This is the crucial part. You may choose a month you like to practice the exercise. You may even repeat the cycle. If your intention is to awaken the knowledge in Venus's aura, the best time to begin will be 29 days before the Venus retrograde period. So, what should you do on the 29th day once you complete the initiation?

## *Meditate to remember the memory of Venus when Venus begins its retrograde motion:*

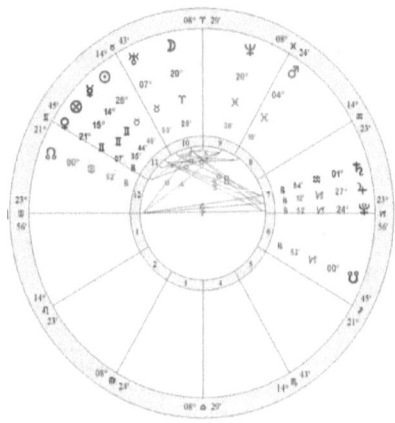

The 1st day of the Venus retrograde period is the first day after you completed the initiation. You first attain the past life memories made available through the gate of the degree of the sign that Venus is in at that time. You will find in the following pages which degrees between 0°-29° correspond to which memories.

Let's assume that Venus retrograde lasts for 40 days including its stationary days. You will be doing the same meditative exercise for each degree during these 40 days. Just focus on the degree, not the sign. Venus might change signs during these 40 days. The signs are not our focus for this exercise.

### *<u>Meditation for the Venus degree activation</u>*:

Venus opens the time corridor in the field of our $2^{nd}$ chakra and transfers the exchange of information through this chakra. The memories of Venus reside here.

Begin the "initiation into emptiness" exercise. When you finally feel yourself at one and complete with everything around you and experience a deep tranquility, remember your emptiness. Keep your focus on your heart chakra. The end of the human is his heart. Let your focus open into the eternity of your being. ***Your heart is where you open yourself into eternity.*** The duality ceases there.

You don't have shadows there. Nothing that belongs to "the outer" can go inside. It doesn't have the power to go inside. You just continue to focus on your heart by taking calm and deep breaths. After a while, you will feel a great pleasure in your heart that expands to your back. At that very moment you achieve to be 'out of time' at the least, you will have met the eternity itself. It is not easy to understand. It doesn't look like anything.

It just is. And it will create such a great pleasure in the body only to stand at the threshold of that eternity. The rest is emptiness. You are at a point where time no longer exists. Focus on your "end", the threshold of your eternity. Give yourself a few moments to experience it when this great pleasure flourishes in your heart chakra. Then take this energy of high pleasure and let it flow down into your second chakra. Continue with the exercise if the energy appears as a pure light in your mind.

Everything is okay. Continue by taking calm and deep breaths. Do not use music for this exercise. The secret of its success is doing it in silence. Stay silent and make sure everything around you is silent as well. *You* should be silent in the first place. Only then time will *stop*. And you will reach the threshold of eternity. Do this exercise for 40 days until the Venus retrograde period is over. Stay in that great pleasure in your heart chakra. You don't have to think, imagine, desire or do anything. Just be silent and let the pleasure flow into your Venus chakra. Just witness it. The rest is Mother Earth's work. Just focus on ***aligning with the Venus retrograde***. That's enough!

From the first day on, you will experience very interesting incidents or meet interesting people depending on the degree Venus begins its retrograde motion in your chart. Make sure you keep a journal where you write about your experiences during these 40 days. I strongly advise you to write. You will be astonished to see what your personal story tells you at the end of the 40th day when you read your journal and realize the energy you awakened.

You will grasp in your writing the specific Venusian problem you should work on with your Hermetic astrologer. You will be working on the right issue so that you can transform it into a friendly and positive energy. It is one thing to say *"I want to love myself"*; and it is another thing to be able to state "I lived these experiences because of a promise I could not keep or a responsivity I took in a past life.

I know that I brought what I could not forgive into this life, as a shadow."
Now you have your Venus issue in a concrete, definite and clear form. You can work on it to neutralize the energy. And it will definitely bring you success. You will succeed to transform the energy, that used to sabotage you, into love. The sabotager will tend to transform into an energy that supports you in a friendly way.

This friendly support will only continue when you practice the follow-up exercises. The follow-up exercises will be in the second volume of this book, in which I will also share with you the testimonials. You will be reading the results of the exercises which express the incredible transformative power of Hermetic Astrology..

*Meditate to remember the memory of Mars when Mars begins its retrograde motion:*

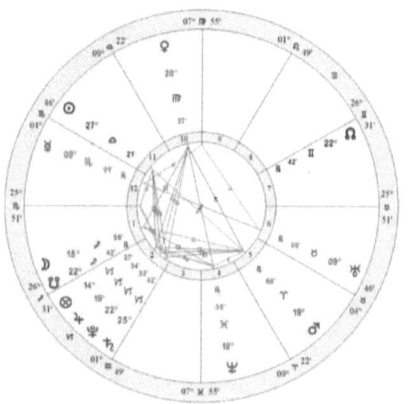

You should apply the same steps you did for the Venus degree activation meditation explained above. The only difference is that Mars is your 1st chakra field and you should let the energy of that great pleasure flow into the field of your 1st chakra.

Mars retrograde lasts for about 60-80 days every two years. (I take it to be 70 days as an average.) It means that you should be doing this exercise for at least 20 minutes every day during those 70 days. Write in your journal all the memories that awaken as you experience your "around the world in 70 days". Work on a specific subject with your consultant and move on by neutralizing the memories that sabotage you.

*Meditate to remember the memory of Mercury when Mercury begins its retrograde motion:*

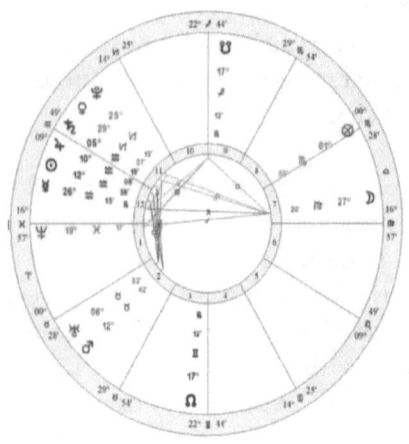

You should apply the same steps you did for the Venus degree activation meditation. The only difference is that Mercury is your 5th chakra field and this time you should let the energy of that great pleasure flow into the field of your 5th chakra.

Mercury retrograde lasts for about 20 days which means that you should be doing this exercise for at least 20 minutes every day during those 20 days.

Write in your journal all the memories that awaken in 20 days. Work on a specific subject with your consultant and move on by neutralizing the memories that sabotage you.

*Meditate to remember the memory of Jupiter when Jupiter begins its retrograde motion:*

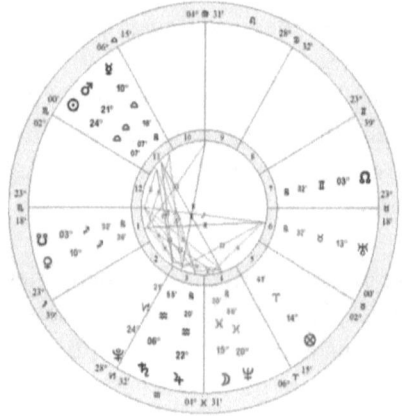

You should apply the same steps you did for the Venus degree activation meditation. The only difference is that Jupiter is your 6th chakra field and you should let the energy of that great pleasure flow into the field of your 6th chakra. Jupiter retrograde lasts for about 120 days which means that you should be doing this exercise for at least 20 minutes every day during those 120 days. Write in your journal all the memories that awaken in 120 days. Work on a specific subject with your consultant and move on by neutralizing the memories that sabotage you.

The exercises might feel long for some of you. No, they are very short actually. I would not advise you to begin these exercises just to give it a try based on curiosity or a sense of adventure. However, if you take yourself serious enough to pursue your *reason* to live, I would advise you to have a disciplined approach. These are not exercises for "having a try". I am not offering you a personal development or motivational tool. These exercises will not put up with a "let's try and see what happens" approach. Either *do* them or do not start at all!

All the planets see through our hearts when they look at us. So does the Moon. Planets reflect back to our hearts the information they had taken into their chakras by sending their light of their own time to our hearts. So ***while a planet is transferring information to one of our chakras or receiving information from them, it reaches us from the threshold of our end.*** For example, Venus cannot transfer its light to our second chakra directly from the time corridor that it opens. The time corridor always connects to our heart chakra first. And it expands from there into other chakras of our bodies. So Venus first opens a time corridor into our heart chakra and then reaches the field of our second chakra. ***No light will ever move randomly.***

***Our hearts do not function in duality.*** Our heart chakra is the only chakra that does not function according to the duality principle. That is why it is ***the endpoint of human***. What you have here is a great pleasure and peace. ***This is not a place that is created by duality; on the contrary, it is where duality cannot enter. Because there is nowhere to enter. It is the threshold of eternity in our bodies.***

Each moving object in universe connect to another through their hearts. ***The heart, namely the center or threshold, is the main center where the knowledge of the memory is found in.***

This is the threshold one can arrive once two opposites are united. You can't arrive such a threshold by taking sides. That is why your shadow does not exist in the End of the Earth. Neither do you. The two of you unite and turn into something else at that point. That is how the threshold becomes visible for you. When you and your shadow unite in order to arrive a certain threshold, what arises is nothing but contentment. Therefore, you can only understand what *combining, integrating* or *metamorphosing* is when you feel content. When you are content, you know that you begin to experience *being whole*. And this is the purpose of all these exercises; feeling whole and complete.

## Dreams of Remembering:

We call the phase when we don't see the Moonlight in the sky as "New Moon". When the Moon is not in the sky, it transfers the memory it received from us to Pluto. When this New Moon phase takes place in your $9^{th}$ and $12^{th}$ houses, you can use the dreams you see during the 2 days when Moon is in that particular house. Try to do this exercise at nighttime.

That is why I suggest that you make an intention to see a dream of remembering when the Moon is not in the sky. The dreams of remembering are different than the dreams you see in other times. They are dreams that you can remember with great details when you are awake. There will always a symbol, a name etc. that is almost imprinted in your mind. Such dreams have content and you do not forget them. If you forget about your dream, which you think is a dream of remembering, you should know that it is actually an activity arranged by your daily life. You don't feel tired when you awake from a real dream of remembering. It never makes you feel bad. Neither do you feel an intense excitement or hurry etc. You feel very calm and moderate.

*"Man is the will of the Earth and Sky"*

**Remember**

*Remember*

# CHAPTER I

The main purpose of the retrograde motion is to help us to incarnate in the easiest way possible. This is the deepest meaning of retrograde. ***We are the end results of a need***. The Earth needs us to be healthy; it needs us to incarnate and progress in our evolution easily. The planets influence our incarnation process through their direct and retrograde motion. And they do this on a regular basis. Because they need the data we produce through our power of thought. And they need the retrograde movement in order to transfer this data. ***The karmic memory that we create during the incarnation process are their nourishment in a way. In other words, the planets need the energy (the time, i.e. the karmic memory) that we produce so that they can incarnate in a healthy and continuous way.*** That is why the planets are 'nourished' by the Earth to a great degree. Retrograde periods are the most efficient times for the planets. Each planet that affects us incarnates with us. Therefore we might be meeting the needs of the Earth as well as that of our own beings when we incarnate on Earth. However, we are already incarnated in different vibrations or manifestations in the aura of each planet that take parts in this story. We might not have a body on these planets like we have here. Yet we somehow live on all of these planets. That is how our different parts can have a continuous connection with us in this life. If we collect all of our parts that are incarnated on other planets, we will be one and whole. ***As a part of our being has a 'well-being' here in this life, being incarnated on Earth, other parts of us will be well too.***

There are cycles of memory transfer since our parts can connect with us during each retrograde period. Because **each memory is an energy that we produce. It is just like a fuel. This fuel is knowledge.** We don't know where in the universe this knowledge functions as a *nucleus knowledge* for the formation of a star. It always happened the same way. The thoughts you produce do not linger around freely. They each are a source of power and we don't know what they generate in the universe. Imagine it this way; if you can't create an energy of thought here; your version that is incarnated on Venus as a 'dust cloud', will not be able to turn into a sky comet in time. Therefore, I suggest that we live with a healthy body and produce healthy thoughts.

Each planet has a time cycle and we are beings that awaken in *time* itself. We are in a time travel each and every moment, being both the traveler, path and knowledge all at once. ***Retrograde motion signifies the connection between the common time and different corridors of time.*** And we experience this activity as a sense of "slowing down" in time. Nevertheless, time does not slow down. It might get faster; but it doesn't slow down. During the retrograde period, the old and new corridors of time become "joint". Because everything that incarnates should be able to realize this function in order to form its "other part" and reinforce it. ***As beings scattered to different levels, we can communicate with other parts of us more easily during the retrograde period.*** Our thoughts keep incarnating on different planets in different ways each and every moment. Therefore ***it is easier to connect with our thoughts that are incarnated out of Earth.***

# The Formula

*The Retrograde Planet and Moon Connection:*

Everything starts with the following questions: Which house is the Moon located? Which degree's memory does it activate?

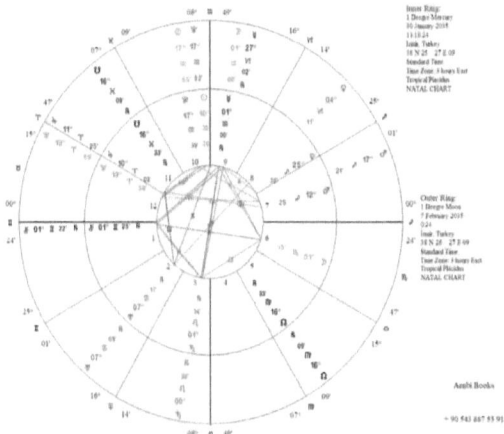

You need to do the following steps for an answer.

*Example:*
Let's assume that Mercury is at 1° in Aquarius (in any house) in the Natal chart. And the Moon has a transit in Aquarius and passes through that particular house at 1°.

*When the Moon at 1° and Mercury at 1° are conjunct, it opens up the 1° memory (time) of the retrograde Mercury. The planet, the dispositor and the aspects of the degree uncover the issue and the solution.*

What starts the karma is Mars and the sign of karma is Capricorn. The Lord of Karma is Saturn and the degrees of karma are 9 and 12. The aspects of karma is conjunction and 90°. Attempting to remember the past life karma is signified by Scorpio; whereas attaining the information of the past life karma is represented by Sagittarius. What unveils the knowledge is Sun. The planets of the attempt of remembering the past life karma are Saturn and Pluto (especially a Pluto that either has a connection or the 12th house). The specific degree and aspect for such an attempt are respectively signified by 9 degrees and an aspect of 90°. You can't make a connection between the two "emptiness", i.e. two states of "timelessness" through an aspect of 180 degree.

180° signifies being "as clear as black and white". On the other hand, half-visibility or half-non-visibility signifies the revelation of the karmic memory. The 90° degree aspect between two different frames of time addresses us; whereas the other 90 degree part addresses to Pluto. ***We should know that when a particular planet, asteroid etc. appears to us at 90°, it reveals its "other 90°degree" part to Pluto.***

The planet in retrograde is transferring all the memory to Pluto through that channel.

Take note of the planets that make a 90° aspect to Mars. Your actions under the influence of this connection will leave a mark in your life, causing a distinct impact on you and the Earth. Once your soul that leaves the physical body arrives at the threshold of Pluto, this information will be transferred to the "information bank" of Pluto in the first following retrograde, to later appear before you. Each soul that achieves to pass through the timelessness (threshold) of Pluto receives a mirror, namely the memories, before coming into this life. And it takes its first breath in a physical body under the influence of a 90° aspect. The 90° in the sky is very crucial during the birth, independently of the faculties of the celestial elements that make the aspect. It is a sign that shows the themes a soul is inclined to remember in a human body.

The aspects of 9° and 90° always indicate that the story of the past life will somehow be remembered. These aspects are gates that open into the past life or the lives before that. The 90° aspect possesses a "retrograde psychology" in terms of remembering. The 90° aspect in a chart represents a field that works just like a retrograde. 12th house is the house of the retrograde wisdom and Pisces is the sign of the retrograde.

*When Mercury is in Retro by transit;* you can easily access the past life information regarding the themes represented by the planet it is conjunct to. Since the conjunction is in Mercury nature, it encourages the karmic remembering regarding the issues represented by the other planet that it conjunct in the natal chart.

*Each sign has a point of remembering:*

Pay attention to the 9° of a sign. It doesn't matter if there is a planet in this sign or not. What is important is that we see the 9° of that sign. There's no -1/+1 tolerance here.

*What does the 9° degree of a sign express?*

For example, as a planet in Aries passes through each degree of the sign, it opens the memory that the degree transfers from the past lives into the current one. Mercury, for example, awakens all the memory that was recorded in the time corridor that corresponds to this specific date in your previous lifetime when it is at 5° Aries. Therefore, you can access the records. As you see, you do not need to wait for Mercury to be at 9° to "remember". You can think of the 9° as a hole in a blown-up balloon or the door of a room that can be opened. Each degree, including the 0°-29, has a memory. ***Each one of the total 360 degrees is a field where different memories are recorded.***

***If the house is compared to a room in the natal chart, the gate of that room is always the 9°.*** This is the entrance of the house in terms of karmic remembering. Karmic information goes in and out of the 9th gate. The action should be realized under the influence of the 90° aspect for the information to reach the 9th gate. The experience may last days. The information that comes out of an intentional action gradually becomes concentrated due to the repetition of thoughts and actions. It is an accumulation which constitutes a memory. A concentration between 0°-90° is required for this memory to be turned into a "definite record". The total 90° is like 90 days. Let us examine the value of 9 more closely:

*If you do something at least for 20 minutes every day during 90 days, "its degree" will be 90.*

*90 days × 20 minutes = 1800 minutes*
*1800 minutes ÷ 20 minutes = 90°*
*If the aspect is 90°;*
*20 minutes × 90° = 1800*
*1800 ÷ 20 minutes = 90°.*

*The karmic value of 90 days is 24 hours 1440 minutes. If we add the digits, we get 1+4+4+0=9.*
*1440 minutes × 90 days=129.600 minutes.*
*If we add these digits:*
*1+2+9+6+0+0=18*
*1+8=9*

## Receiving information from 9° Aries in your natal chart:

We should carefully understand the relations of Mars, the dispositor of Aries, in the natal chart. Write down how many of the following properties Mars has.

1. Is Mars in 9°?  -/+1 degree is not tolerated.
2. Is Mars in the 9th house?
3. If not, does it have an aspect with any of the planets or other astrological elements in the 9th house?
4. Is Mars in the 9th sign?
5. If not, does it have any aspect with the planets or other astrological elements in the 9th sign?
6. Does Mars have a 90° aspect with Jupiter?
7. If not, does it have a 90° aspect with Jupiter's dispositor?
8. Is Mars in Sagittarius?
9. If not, how is Mars related to Sagittarius?
10. Does Mars have an aspect with any of the planets or other astrological elements at 9°?
11. Does Mars make an aspect with the gatekeeper of the south, the Fomalhaut? ( Because it is the fixed star

Fomalhaut that is exposed to the total energy of the 9°.)

12. Does Mars make a 90° aspect with a planet or other astrological element that is related to Fomalhaut?

13. Does Mars have an aspect with a planet that has a 90° aspect to Fomalhaut?

In short; when deciphering the karma through the story Mars awakens, we need to look at the 9th house, Sagittarius, Jupiter, any planet at , even if Mars is not in the 9th house. Does any planet with a 90 degree angle to Mars send you to the story there?

So this is the place where the stories that will be reminded by Mars are recorded. Mars easily opens the celestial gates on these points. It does that with willingness and enthusiasm.

*** Because it is a savior due to its nature. ***

### *Receiving information from 9° Taurus in your natal chart:*

We should carefully understand the relations of Venus, the dispositor of Taurus, in the natal chart. Write down how many of the following properties Venus has.

1. Is Venus in 9°? -/+1 degree is not tolerated.
2. Is Venus in the 9$^{th}$ house?
3. If not, does it have an aspect with any of the planets or other astrological elements in the 9$^{th}$ house?
4. Is Venus in the 9$^{th}$ sign?
5. If not, does it have any aspect with the planets or other astrological elements in the 9$^{th}$ sign?
6. Does Venus have a 90° aspect with Jupiter?
7. If not, does it have a 90° aspect with Jupiter's dispositor?
8. Is Venus in Sagittarius?
9. If not, how is Venus related to Sagittarius?
10. Does Venus have an aspect with any of the planets or other astrological elements at 9°?
11. Does Venus make an aspect with the gatekeeper of the south, the Fomalhaut? (Because it is the fixed star Fomalhaut that is exposed to the total energy of the 9°.)

12. Does Venus make a 90° aspect with a planet or other astrological element that is related to Fomalhaut?

13. Does Venus have an aspect with a planet that has a 90° aspect to Fomalhaut?

In short; when deciphering your karma with the story Venus awakens, we need to check the following: Does Venus point a 90 degree aspect between a celestial element and another one in the 9th house, in Sagittarius, at 9 degrees or Jupiter?

So this is the place where the stories that will be reminded by Venus are recorded. Venus opens the celestial gates on these points easily. Because *it is matter due to its nature. So to say, it is a result of the karma.*

## Receiving information from the 9th degree of Gemini in your Natal Chart

We should carefully understand the relations of Mercury, the dispositor of Gemini, in the natal chart. Write down how many of the following properties Mercury has.

1. Is Mercury at 9°? -/+1 degree is not tolerated.
2. Is Mercury in the 9th house?
3. If not, does it have an aspect with any of the planets or other astrological elements in the 9th house?
4. Is Mercury in the 9th sign?
5. If not, does it have any aspect with the planets or other astrological elements in the 9th sign?
6. Does Mercury have a 90° aspect with Jupiter?
7. If not, does it have a 90° aspect with Jupiter's dispositor?
8. Is Mercury in Sagittarius?
9. If not, how is Mercury related to Sagittarius?
10. Does Mercury have an aspect with any of the planets or other astrological elements at 9°?
11. Does Mercury make an aspect with the gatekeeper of the south, the Fomalhaut? (Because it is the fixed star

Fomalhaut that is exposed to the total energy of the 9°.)

12. Does Mercury make a 90° aspect with a planet or other astrological element that is related to Fomalhaut?

13. Does Mercury have an aspect with a planet that has a 90° aspect to Fomalhaut?

In short; when deciphering your karma with the story Mercury awakens, we need to check the following: Does Venus point a 90 degree aspect between a celestial element and another one in the 9th house, in Sagittarius, at 9 degrees or Jupiter?

So this is the place where the stories that will be reminded by Mercury are recorded. Mercury opens the celestial gates on these points easily. Because *it signifies reaching knowledge due to its nature. The knowledge of karma...*

## *Receiving information from 9° Aries in your natal chart:*

We should carefully understand the relations of Moon, the dispositor of Cancer, in the natal chart. Write down how many of the following properties Moon has.

1. Is Moon at 9°? -/+1 degree is not tolerated.
2. Is Moon in the 9th house?
3. If not, does it have an aspect with any of the planets or other astrological elements in the 9th house?
4. Is Moon in the 9th sign? (applicable to the Placidus house system)
5. If not, does it have any aspect with the planets or other astrological elements in the 9th sign?
6. Does Moon have a 90° aspect with Jupiter?
7. If not, does it have a 90° aspect with Jupiter's dispositor?
8. Is Moon in Sagittarius?
9. If not, how is Moon related to Sagittarius?
10. Does Moon have an aspect with any of the planets or other astrological elements at 9°?
11. Does Moon make an aspect with the gatekeeper of the south, the Fomalhaut? ( Because it is the fixed star

Fomalhaut that is exposed to the total energy of the 9°.)

12. Does Moon make a 90° aspect with a planet or other astrological element that is related to Fomalhaut?

13. Does Moon have an aspect with a planet that has a 90° aspect to Fomalhaut?

In short; when deciphering your karma with the story Moon awakened, we need to check the following: Does Moon point a 90 degree aspect between a celestial element and another one in the 9th house, in Sagittarius, at 9 degrees or Jupiter?

So this is the place where the stories that will be reminded by Moon are recorded. Moon opens the celestial gates on these points. Due to its nature, it transfers the knowledge of life on Earth, which is the knowledge of karma, to the *End of the Earth*. ***Just like the first light is Sun, it is the Moon's light that carries the first moment of the first light, each time, to the end of life.***

## _Receiving information from 9° Leo in your natal chart:_

We should carefully understand the relations of Sun, the dispositor of Leo, in the natal chart. Write down how many of the following properties Sun has.

1. Is Sun at 9°?  -/+1 degree is not tolerated.
2. Is Sun in the 9$^{th}$ house?
3. If not, does it have an aspect with any of the planets or other astrological elements in the 9$^{th}$ house?
4. Is Sun in the 9$^{th}$ sign?
5. If not, does it have any aspect with the planets or other astrological elements in the 9$^{th}$ sign?
6. Does Sun have a 90° aspect with Jupiter?
7. If not, does it have a 90° aspect with Jupiter's dispositor?
8. Is Sun in Sagittarius?
9. If not, how is Sun related to Sagittarius?
10. Does Sun have an aspect with any of the planets or other astrological elements at 9°?
11. Does Sun make an aspect with the gatekeeper of the south, the Fomalhaut? ( Because it is the fixed star Fomalhaut that is exposed to the total energy of the 9°.)

12. Does Sun make a 90° aspect with a planet or other astrological element that is related to Fomalhaut?

13. Does Sun have an aspect with a planet that has a 90° aspect to Fomalhaut?

In short; when deciphering your karma with the story Moon awakened, we need to check the following: Does Moon point a 90 degree aspect between a celestial element and another one in the 9th house, in Sagittarius, at 9 degrees or Jupiter?

So this is the place where the stories that will be reminded by Sun are recorded. Sun opens the celestial gates on these points easily. ***Due to its nature, it is the first light of the life on Earth. It is the first light. First light of the life…***

### Receiving information from 9° Virgo in your natal chart:

We should carefully understand the relations of Mercury, the dispositor of Virgo, in the natal chart. Write down how many of the following properties Mercury has.

1. Is Mercury at 9°? -/+1 degree is not tolerated.
2. Is Mercury in the 9th house?
3. If not, does it have an aspect with any of the planets or other astrological elements in the 9th house?
4. Is Mercury in the 9th sign?
5. If not, does it have any aspect with the planets or other astrological elements in the 9th sign?
6. Does Mercury have a 90° aspect with Jupiter?
7. If not, does it have a 90° aspect with Jupiter's dispositor?
8. Is Mercury in Sagittarius?
9. If not, how is Mercury related to Sagittarius?
10. Does Mercury have an aspect with any of the planets or other astrological elements at 9°?
11. Does Mercury make an aspect with the gatekeeper of the south, the Fomalhaut? ( Because it is the fixed star

Fomalhaut that is exposed to the total energy of the 9°.)

12. Does Mercury make a 90° aspect with a planet or other astrological element that is related to Fomalhaut?

13. Does Mercury have an aspect with a planet that has a 90° aspect to Fomalhaut?

In short; when deciphering your karma with the story Mercury awakened, we need to check the following: Does Mercury point a 90 degree aspect between a celestial element and another one in the 9th house, in Sagittarius, at 9 degrees or Jupiter?

So this is the place where the stories that will be reminded by Mercury are recorded. Mercury opens the celestial gates on these points easily. *Due to its nature, it is the energy that starts the process of measuring and evaluating the functions of the karmic information.*

### Receiving information from 9° Libra in your natal chart:

We should carefully understand the relations of Venus, the dispositor of Libra, in the natal chart. Write down how many of the following properties Venus has.

1. Is Venus at 9°? -/+1 degree is not tolerated.
2. Is Venus in the 9$^{th}$ house?
3. If not, does it have an aspect with any of the planets or other astrological elements in the 9$^{th}$ house?
4. Is Venus in the 9$^{th}$ sign?
5. If not, does it have any aspect with the planets or other astrological elements in the 9$^{th}$ sign?
6. Does Venus have a 90° aspect with Jupiter?
7. If not, does it have a 90° aspect with Jupiter's dispositor?
8. Is Venus in Sagittarius?
9. If not, how is Venus related to Sagittarius?
10. Does Venus have an aspect with any of the planets or other astrological elements at 9°?
11. Does Venus make an aspect with the gatekeeper of the south, the Fomalhaut? (Because it is the fixed star Fomalhaut that is exposed to the total energy of the 9°.)

12. Does Venus make a 90° aspect with a planet or other astrological element that is related to Fomalhaut?

13. Does Venus have an aspect with a planet that has a 90° aspect to Fomalhaut?

In short; when deciphering your karma with the story Venus awakened, we need to check the following: Does Venus point a 90 degree aspect between a celestial element and another one in the 9th house, in Sagittarius, at 9 degrees or Jupiter?

So this is the place where the stories that will be reminded by Venus are recorded. Venus opens the celestial gates on these points easily. *Due to its nature, it is the first energy that can achieve to be the channel receives the "anger" from Pluto and transfer it as "justice" into life. It is the female of the parents of the threshold of the End of the Earth.* I will be publishing a book about this particular role of Venus. It is vital to understand Venus.

### _Receiving information from 9° Scorpio in your natal chart:_

We should carefully understand the relations of Mars and Pluto, the dispositors of Scorpio, in the natal chart. Write down how many of the following properties Mars and Pluto have.

1. Are Mars and Pluto at 9°? -/+1 degree is not tolerated.

2. Are Mars and Pluto in the 9th house?

3. If not, do they have an aspect with any of the planets or other astrological elements in the 9th house?

4. Are Mars and Pluto in the 9th sign?

5. If not, do they have any aspect with the planets or other astrological elements in the 9th sign?

6. Do Mars and Pluto have a 90° aspect with Jupiter?

7. If not, do they have a 90° aspect with Jupiter's dispositor?

8. Are Mars and Pluto in Sagittarius?

9. If not, how are Mars and Pluto related to Sagittarius?

10. Do Mars and Pluto have an aspect with any of the planets or other astrological elements at 9°?

11. Do Mars and Pluto make an aspect with the gatekeeper of the south,

the Fomalhaut? (Because it is the fixed star Fomalhaut that is exposed to the total energy of the 9°.)

12. Do Mars and Pluto make a 90° aspect with a planet or other astrological element that is related to Fomalhaut?

13. Do Mars and Pluto have an aspect with a planet that has a 90° aspect to Fomalhaut?

In short; when deciphering your karma with the story Mars and Pluto awakened, we need to check the following: Do Mars and Pluto point a 90 degree aspect between a celestial element and another one in the 9th house, in Sagittarius, at 9 degrees or Jupiter?

So this is the place where the stories that will be reminded by Mars and Pluto are recorded. Mars and Pluto open the celestial gates on these points. ***Because, by their nature, they have the secret of the power born out of the dynamic of anger. And they know that this power triggers life. By the way, only Pluto has the secret. Because Mars is one of the planets that emerges as the secret itself instead of keeping the secret. Yet it is unaware that it is a secret. Mars in Scorpio is very different from the Mars in Aries.*** I plan to publish a book on this specific Mars in the future.

### Receiving information from 9° Sagittarius in your natal chart:

We will examine Jupiter and Chiron respectively. We should carefully understand the relations of Jupiter, the dispositor of Sagittarius, in the natal chart. Write down how many of the following properties Jupiter has.

1. Is Jupiter at 9°? -/+1 degree is not tolerated.
2. Is Jupiter in the 9$^{th}$ house?
3. If not, does it have an aspect with any of the planets or other astrological elements in the 9$^{th}$ house?
4. Is Jupiter in the 9$^{th}$ sign?
5. If not, does it have any aspect with the planets or other astrological elements in the 9$^{th}$ sign?
6. Does Jupiter have a 90° aspect with Jupiter?
7. If not, does it have a 90° aspect with Jupiter's dispositor?
8. Is Jupiter in Sagittarius?
9. If not, how is Jupiter related to Sagittarius?
10. Does Jupiter have an aspect with any of the planets or other astrological elements at 9°?
11. Does Jupiter make an aspect with the gatekeeper of the south, the Fomalhaut? (Because it is the fixed star

Fomalhaut that is exposed to the total energy of the 9°.)

12. Does Jupiter make a 90° aspect with a planet or other astrological element that is related to Fomalhaut?

13. Does Jupiter have an aspect with a planet that has a 90° aspect to Fomalhaut?

In short; when deciphering your karma with the story Jupiter awakened, we need to check the following: Does Jupiter point a 90 degree aspect between a celestial element and another one in the 9th house, in Sagittarius, at 9 degrees or Jupiter?

So this is the place where the stories that will be reminded by Jupiter are recorded. Jupiter opens the celestial gates on these points easily. For *it is the first force that can honestly approach the relationship between the owner of the 'first voice' and his son, which by nature awakens the universe. It is the powerful energy of Jupiter who knows and respects the secret in the adventure of initiating the first time corridor on this Earth, and takes an honest attitude for the fight between Saturn and Uranus.*

## *Let us examine Chiron closer to receive information from 9° Sagittarius in your Natal Chart*

We should carefully understand the relations of Chiron in the natal chart. Write down how many of the following properties Chiron has.

1. Is Chiron at 9°? -/+1 degree is not tolerated.
2. Is Chiron in the 9<sup>th</sup> house?
3. If not, does it have an aspect with any of the planets or other astrological elements in the 9<sup>th</sup> house?
4. Is Chiron in the 9<sup>th</sup> sign?
5. If not, does it have any aspect with the planets or other astrological elements in the 9<sup>th</sup> sign?
6. Does Chiron have a 90° aspect with Jupiter?
7. If not, does it have a 90° aspect with Jupiter's dispositor?
8. Is Chiron in Sagittarius?
9. If not, how is Chiron related to Sagittarius?
10. Does Chiron have an aspect with any of the planets or other astrological elements at 9°?
11. Does Chiron make an aspect with the gatekeeper of the south, the Fomalhaut? (Because it is the fixed star

Fomalhaut that is exposed to the total energy of the 9°.)

12. Does Chiron make a 90° aspect with a planet or other astrological element that is related to Fomalhaut?

13. Does Chiron have an aspect with a planet that has a 90° aspect to Fomalhaut?

In short; when deciphering your karma with the story Jupiter awakened, we need to check the following: Does Chiron point a 90 degree aspect between a celestial element and another one in the 9th house, in Sagittarius, at 9 degrees or Jupiter?

So this is the place where the stories that will be reminded by Chiron are recorded. Chiron opens the celestial gates on these points. Because *he is the symbol of sacrifice, which, by its nature, witnesses the relationship between the owner of the 'first voice' that awakens the universe and his son. Chiron can transform the energy that arises from the fight into healing. He closely experiences this Earth as well as the two most important sources of conflict from which celestial time corridors are created. Chiron witnesses the birth of time moment by moment due to his celestial position.*

<u>Receiving information from 9° Aries in your natal chart:</u>

We should carefully understand the relations of Saturn, the dispositor of Capricorn, in the natal chart. Write down how many of the following properties Saturn has.

1. Is Saturn at 9°? -/+1 degree is not tolerated.
2. Is Saturn in the 9th house?
3. If not, does it have an aspect with any of the planets or other astrological elements in the 9th house?
4. Is Saturn in the 9th sign?
5. If not, does it have any aspect with the planets or other astrological elements in the 9th sign?
6. Does Saturn have a 90° aspect with Jupiter?
7. If not, does it have a 90° aspect with Jupiter's dispositor?
8. Is Saturn in Sagittarius?
9. If not, how is Saturn related to Sagittarius?
10. Does Saturn have an aspect with any of the planets or other astrological elements at 9°?
11. Does Saturn make an aspect with the gatekeeper of the south, the Fomalhaut? (Because it is the fixed star Fomalhaut that is exposed to the total energy of the 9°.)

12. Does Saturn make a 90° aspect with a planet or other astrological element that is related to Fomalhaut?

13. Does Saturn have an aspect with a planet that has a 90° aspect to Fomalhaut?

In short; when deciphering your karma with the story Saturn awakened, we need to check the following: Does Saturn point a 90 degree aspect between a celestial element and another one in the 9th house, in Sagittarius, at 9 degrees or Jupiter?

So this is the place where the stories that will be reminded by Saturn are recorded. Saturn opens the celestial gates on these points. Because *it is the son of the owner of the 'first voice' which, by its nature, awakens the universe. It controls the first phase of life after the 'first sound' and the transformation of the 'first light' into a soul. So it has the secret of the soul's entrance into our system.*

## Receiving information from 9° Aries in your natal chart:

We should carefully understand the relations of Uranus and Saturn, the dispositors of Aquarius, in the natal chart. Write down how many of the following properties Uranus and Saturn have.

1. Are Uranus and Saturn at 9°? -/+1 degree is not tolerated.
2. Are Uranus and Saturn in the 9th house?
3. If not, do they have an aspect with any of the planets or other astrological elements in the 9th house?
4. Are Uranus and Saturn in the 9th sign?
5. If not, do they have any aspect with the planets or other astrological elements in the 9th sign?
6. Do Uranus and Saturn have a 90° aspect with Jupiter?
7. If not, do they have a 90° aspect with Jupiter's dispositor?
8. Are Uranus and Saturn in Sagittarius?
9. If not, how are Uranus and Saturn related to Sagittarius?
10. Do Uranus and Saturn have an aspect with any of the planets or other astrological elements at 9°?

11. Do Uranus and Saturn make an aspect with the gatekeeper of the south, the Fomalhaut? (Because it is the fixed star Fomalhaut that is exposed to the total energy of the 9°.)

12. Do Uranus and Saturn make a 90° aspect with a planet or other astrological element that is related to Fomalhaut?

13. Do Uranus and Saturn have an aspect with a planet that has a 90° aspect to Fomalhaut?

In short; when deciphering your karma with the story Saturn awakens, we need to check the following: Does Saturn point a 90 degree aspect between a celestial element and another one in the 9th house, in Sagittarius, at 9 degrees or Jupiter?

Here are your stories that Uranus and Saturn will remind you. Uranus and Saturn open the celestial gates at these points. Because *they are 'first' by nature. They have the secrets of the direction in the universe you come from and the time corridors you moved through to reach Earth. They are two great forces that hold the first secret of all known creation. Uranus-Saturn is the first known father-son dilemma in the universe. The universe was not born out of a combination of female and male powers. It has come into being through the 'sound'. The universe was subsequently divided into two in order to perpetuate itself. Sinlessness has produced the universe, not a male-female power. The universe has no gender. Gender is a creation on our planet which belongs to the son that takes Uranus away from us. Gender begins in 'time'. Gender is specific to us. From the father-son dilemma, you begin to remember the origins of your spiritual precession rather than your personal history. That remembrance connects you with your being that came before your experience on Earth. So what were you and where were you before you came here as a soul and took a human body? They establish your connection with those versions at any moment. They derive their power from such a faculty.*

### Receiving information from 9° Pisces in your natal chart:

We should carefully understand the relations of Jupiter and Neptune, the dispositors of Pisces, in the natal chart. Write down how many of the following properties Jupiter and Neptune have.

1. Are Jupiter and Neptune at 9°? -/+1 degree is not tolerated.

2. Are Jupiter and Neptune in the 9$^{th}$ house?

3. If not, do they have an aspect with any of the planets or other astrological elements in the 9$^{th}$ house?

4. Are Jupiter and Neptune in the 9$^{th}$ sign?

5. If not, do they have any aspect with the planets or other astrological elements in the 9$^{th}$ sign?

6. Do Jupiter and Neptune have a 90° aspect with Jupiter?

7. If not, do they have a 90° aspect with Jupiter's dispositor?

8. Are Jupiter and Neptune in Sagittarius?

9. If not, how are Jupiter and Neptune related to Sagittarius?

10. Do Jupiter and Neptune have an aspect with any of the planets or other astrological elements at 9°?

11. Do Jupiter and Neptune make an aspect with the gatekeeper of the south, the Fomalhaut? ( Because it is the fixed star Fomalhaut that is exposed to the total energy of the 9°.)

12. Do Jupiter and Neptune make a 90° aspect with a planet or other astrological element that is related to Fomalhaut?

13. Do Jupiter and Neptune have an aspect with a planet that has a 90° aspect to Fomalhaut?

In short; when deciphering your karma with the story Jupiter and Neptune awakened, we need to check the following: Do Jupiter and Neptune point a 90 degree aspect between a celestial element and another one in the 9th house, in Sagittarius, at 9 degrees or Jupiter?

Here are your stories that Jupiter and Neptune will remind you. Jupiter and Neptune open the celestial gates at these points. Because **by their nature, in Pisces, they signify the gate of humanity that opens into the universe.**

# Degrees for Karmic Remembering

Now, I would like to explain the "karmic degrees of remembering", which are indicators for significant purposes. I will present you *the information which will enable you to distinguish natives who, by birth, have the potential to reach their karmic memory at any time, without requiring a special initiation into alchemy, hermeticism or esoteric work.* When you see any planets at the following special degrees in a natal chart, continue to work on the chart keeping this information in your mind. You are consulting a person who naturally remembers, without needing an initiation. Such **rememberers are also 'natural' reminders.**

The related degrees are: 9°- 18°- 27°

Check the natal chart. Which of the planets are at least at one of these degrees? Sometimes, 3 different planets might be at exactly these degrees. This is not a requirement though. It is enough to have a planet at either 9°, 18° or 27° in the chart. It indicates that this person is a natural rememberer and reminder. Such people invoke the past for anything they touch in nature, only by their existence. Pay attention to their studies on reincarnation. Because they *know* it.

*Let us now review the technical information for the degrees;*

**9°;** Chiron's degree of exaltation in Gemini

**18°;** Based on my research on astrology, esoterism and Hermeticism, I notice that there is a powerful star which I think will smile to us, who are on Earth, a few ages later in the cycle of the karmic memory. And 18° is the degree of exaltation for this powerful star. What is meant by exaltation here is representation. Therefore, this fixed star, which has been accepted as the representative of "Endless Goodness" for thousands of years, can appear to us at 18° in Sagittarius. "Endless Goodness" is a fixed star that was believed to be where Prophet Zoroaster had come from thousands of years ago. It will be viewed purple in color from the Earth. When this fixed star us establishes a direct connection with us, humanity will be on the brink of a completely different age. With the guidance of this fixed star, humanity will be able to carry his past into the future.

**27°;** the degree of exaltation in Pisces for Venus

How should we perceive *9°, 18° and 27°* in their own right?

It is essential to check the relations of these degrees in the natal chart.

Which planets are at 9°, 18° or 27°? Do they have a connection to Chiron, Venus and Aura? Chiron represents the memory of Uranus and Saturn. Venus represents the memory of Pluto. Chiron possesses the secret of the awakening of the universe. Venus, possesses the consciousness that expands through the Centre of the World.

There is a consciousness that evolves through the secret of the *End of the Earth* and Venus has it.

*I would like to teach you the houses whose stories can be remembered most easily;*

If the cusp of a house in your natal chart begins with 9°, 18°, 27°, it indicates that the memory of this house can easily be activated. The activation is determined by planet transits.

## The Nines:
Mercury, Venus, Earth, Mars, Jupiter, Saturn, Uranus, Neptune, Pluto

9° of each sign is a gate that opens into the past and present. We should take note where the 9th house opens to. Therefore we can track the memories that will be uncovered and where their energy will touch. This "tracking" will give you a tremendous feeling of joy. Let me illustrate it with an example. Ascendant is in Scorpio, let us find the 9° of Scorpio. If the native has his ASC at 14° in Scorpio, its 9° will be found in the 12th house. You can also specify the place of the 9° by counting back, starting from the 14°.

The 12th house of a native is the house of his past in its own right. Entering into the past and exiting into the present is done through this gate of 9. Since it is the 9° Scorpio that signifies the gate that opens into the past, the exchange of this information has the nature of Scorpio's scenario. This person knows the impossibility of death; the possibility and easiness of time travel as well as the transition between lifetimes. He knows that such phenomenon do happen each moment. Deep inside, he has known the scenario of Scorpio since his birth.

He does not discover it after being inspired by other things.

A Scorpion memory always possesses the power to know the formation of the reincarnation process; because Scorpio is a scenario related to the *End of the Earth*. That is why you should pay attention to the 9° Scorpio. It is your gate that opens into the *End of the Earth*. We should carefully analyze any Full Moon as well as the Lunar and Solar Eclipses that happen at 9° Scorpio. The secret of death walks among us in those days. They are special days. Please take note that I said not the "death" but "the secret of death comes" in these days. Understanding the activities of Pluto and Mercury in that period will give us awareness.

All the houses, without any exception, are fields that open into the memories of past lives at any moment. Such fields that host the knowledge carry on their function in a regular way. The zodiac has a splendid harmony and music. The zodiac is the field where every particle of the Universe finds a place for itself. And ***all the planets and other celestial bodies that find their places in the Zodiac exist as 'musicians' who together perform the symphony of the universe. Harmony and music are essentially nothing but the memories of the past, present and future.*** This is the unique symphony of being transformed at any moment.

The conductor of this orchestra is unarguably Pluto for our planet, behind the scenes, in any generation. Even though the planetary number of Pluto is nine, it is the $10^{th}$ in the cycle of the reincarnation led by the Moon light. Pluto is in the 9th place when it represents the pure energy of the Earth, i.e. its center. However it is in the 10th when Pluto needs eyes and gets possession of the Sun and Moon in order to act its role in the Moon cycle. A Pluto that possesses eyes can see the light, i.e. the Earth and the sky of the humans. It is Pluto that makes the scene in life. The specialty of the Eye of the Night (Moonlight) is its ability to encompass all the memory until the 9. It has the power to hold together the mission of the Nine and the elements of the harmony that create the symphony in the dance of the Earth and heavens. Pluto does not exhibit typical planetary properties. As a living organism, it has a flexible structure. There is Plutonic energy in each of the houses. I will now show you the original energy of the field that we call a "house" in astrology:

Each house is created as a result of the intertwining of the energies of the 9 planets, except Pluto, in a certain sequence. What we call houses in the zodiac are nothing but intertwined memories (time corridors). The aspects are created between the planets depending on the distances in degrees. It means that degrees function as gates that connect memories from one house to another. Out of this relationship emerges an aspect, in other words "a common memory".

It is the degrees that create the houses. A degree is a gate that opens into the past, present and future. That's all! It is a wonderful level of consciousness. Try to examine the minor and major aspects through the perspective of such a consciousness. You will see which memories are linked together in what way to give birth to an aspect. Which memories create the 90° aspect or the 180°, 120° and all the others?

The gate through which a planet enters a house is fixed and clear. It is very clear to see the planet, the degree of the house this planet carries the memory to and the themes of the memory. 30 gates (0°-29°) come together to constitute a house in the Zodiac. A house is constituted by 0°-29°.

*"The 'time' you create is the necessary fuel for your other "parts" incarnated in other planets to continue their way."*

**Remember**

**GATES**

## Retrograde and Direct Gates

0°-29° are based on the leadership of the Moon light. Because Moon is the "first eye" of the Nine I mention in the book. Without the Moon light, the planets are blind as they take their roles in the reincarnation cycle. You will see the new Nine in the table below. When one examines the reincarnation cycle from the Earth itself, he will see the roles of the Mercury and Venus through the guidance of the Moon light. When they appear on Earth, the guidance of the Moon will continue to work for the underworld. The eyes of the planets will be the Moon and the Sun once Mercury and Venus are on Earth. Which planets are these? Sun is the eye of Mars and Jupiter that shows the past lives to these planets. That is why, in this book, Sun is expressed as the eye of the Mars and Jupiter after karma is created; and then the eye of Saturn and Neptune within the karmic cycle. Pluto uses both Moon and Sun as its eyes. Uranus does not directly need such a light. Uranus indirectly uses the Moon light as its eye through the activation of its daughter Venus, which is important to know. Because you will track the opening of the gates by understanding the aspects depending on the planets that have Sun and Moon as their eyes during the periods of remembering.

**Sun is the mirror of Earth.** They make a 180° aspect. Therefore Sun is the point of satisfaction for the Earth. It is what completes the Earth and makes it whole. The Sun is the "other half" of the Earth with which it strives to unite. Thus, I write Sun, where the Earth normally corresponds to, in the series of the Nine. Earth is represented as the Sun within the Nine.

Moon light is the eye that guides while going towards the *End of the Earth*; whereas Sun becomes the guiding eye while going from the *End of the Earth* back to the field of life. In other words, Moon is the guiding light that takes you to the underworld while Sun is the light that guides on Earth.

What do Sun and Moon express for the Nine? ***The planets are blind. They can't make their incarnations continuous unless there is the Sunlight and the Moonlight.*** That is why the Moon light expresses the eyes of the planets that open into the past. Moonlight acts as a torch for the karmic memories. It is the Moon light that holds our hands and takes us into our past.

***The Nines: Mercury, Venus, Sun, Mars, Jupiter, Saturn, Uranus, Neptune, Pluto***
***10 Gates: Moon and Mercury, Venus, Sun, Mars, Jupiter, Saturn, Uranus, Neptune, Pluto***

1st gate: Moon 0°
2nd gate: Mercury 1°
3rd gate: Venus 2°
4th gate: Sun 3°
5th gate: Mars 4°
6th gate: Jupiter 5°
7th gate: Saturn 6°
8th gate: Uranus 7°
9th gate: Neptune 8°
10th gate: Pluto 9°

**1st GATE:**

0° is the 1st gate of a house. It is always the gate of the Moonlight that opens into past and exists to present. Moon light is the first thing that enters into a sign. Starting from the 0°, a sign gets activated through the Moonlight. It completes its activation at 29° through Pluto's light. Therefore, a particular sign completes its mission when 29° is over. 0° is the Moonlight and the first gate of the karmic memory. Moonlight begins its journey into the past within the scenario of the sign it is located. It uses the same scenario to arrive at the present. It is the Moonlight that first awakens the past life memories. With the help of this awakening, the past life memories experience their first meeting with the Moonlight that is filtered through the present. That is why I taught you the remembering exercises based on moon phases. Which phase do you use to go down into the *threshold of the End of the Earth*. This is an invaluable theme. That particular phase will provide us more information regarding the nature of the theme.

All the systems that we know speak through the moon. Moon acts and functions in the nature of Mercury in the reincarnation cycle. The messenger is Mercury and the one who transmits this message is the Moon. The difference between them is that Moon does this in order to incarnate. On the other hand, Mercury does not have such a mission. Mercury's incarnation process naturally continues as it "forges" the *knowledge of all*.

*We create karma. Because all the universe needs to incarnate. Moon transfers the memory of life to death; it does not transfer death to life. Because death is where vitality ceases. Moon transfers the memory of life to death while Mercury transfers the memory of death to life.*
*This gate is active any moment when you see the Moonlight in the sky. It is only inactive when there is no Moon in the sky.*

## 2nd GATE:

1° is the 2nd gate of a sign. Mercury uses this gate to rise from the underworld to the surface of the Earth. So Mercury comes from the past at 1° of that sign and reaches the present. By definition, 1° is the rising from the threshold of the *End of the Earth* to the surface and entering into the field of life. The memory carried by Mercury goes in and out through the 2nd gate of a particular sign. This gate is not always active. 1° is activated when Mercury is in retrograde and the 2nd gate is opened widely. Mercury enters through this gate and brings all the memories you created in the past onto the Earth. When Mercury is in retrograde, and under the effect of a transit, its activation continues more intensely until the retrograde period is over. When the transit is over, the Gates of the karmic information is closed until a next transit effect. When Mercury brings an information (memory) from the threshold of the *End of the Earth* on the surface of the Earth, it expresses this by performing music.

Mercury does not sing to us. It transforms the memories into a song that a singer will sing. That is how it presents the information. In each retrograde motion, Mercury goes down into the threshold and transforms the related recollections of your karmic memories into songs and music. In this way, it conveys them to humanity. It is always Venus, Uranus's daughter, that sings the song. That is why you should carefully examine the aspects between Venus and the retrograde Mercury. These aspects activate such deep and influential memories that all the karmic information represented and expressed by Venus get activated. You should understand Venus's activities and "whom" it communicates with in the heavens even though Venus might not be in retrograde in that particular period.

### 3rd GATE:

2 ° is the 3rd Gate of a sign. 2°is the gateway of Venus that opens into the past. Venus descends to the memories of the past through the 3rd Gate and rise to the "present" using the same passage. Venus on Earth creates karma as sexuality, love, worldly pleasures, and material wealth. This 'concrete matter' it creates transfers this karma into the future. In your next karma, just like in this life, it goes down as Aphrodite, and rises as Athena. Venus descends into the threshold of the *End of the Earth as* Aphrodite, i.e. passion (love) and pleasure; returns back on Earth as Athena, i.e. love and justice. 3rd Gate is not always active. 2° is activated when Venus is in retrograde. 3rd Gate opens completely. Venus enters from there and takes all the memories you have created in the past and brings them back to Earth. Moreover, when Venus is in retrograde, and under the effect of a transit, its activation continues more intensely until the retrograde period is over.

When the effect is over, it closes until a next influence.

Venus has a long and meaningful story which you will be able to read in the later pages of the book. I suggest you keep the information mentioned above in mind while reading.

### 4th GATE:
3° is the 4<sup>th</sup> Gate of a house. This is the gate where Sun transfers the past. Mars and Jupiter use the Sun as their eyes. They go down through 3° and rise to the "present" using the same passage. Sun is the 4<sup>th</sup> element in the mathematics of the Zodiac. (Moon-Mercury-Venus-Sun. Because Earth is at the center in the Zodiac.) Earth is the 4<sup>th</sup> in the sequence of the planets & lights in terms of their distances to Sun. (Moon-Mercury-Venus-Earth) At this point, I should elaborate on this subject.

There is always the Earth opposite to Sun. A planet always looks into what is opposite to it, which is actually its mirror. The first light, Sun, sees itself in the Earth. Therefore, first of all, Earth is the mirror of the Sun. The sun sees itself in the Earth. And they create karma towards completion. In this way, they incarnate. This is where the secret lies. ***Reincarnation arises from the relationship between Sun and Earth, which seem different but essentially constitute a whole. So in the first sense, the Earth is the mirror of the Sun. And the Earth sees itself in the sun, its mirror.*** Yet this mission of "being a mirror" first belongs to the Earth. Earth is the mirror of the Sun. ***Earth is the physical body of the Sun.*** Earth grounds the Sun. Looking from a larger perspective, you can see that each planet describes a body and chakra of the Sun. Sun is the mirror of the Earth.

Sun enables the Earth to see itself. Being a fourth gate to a house expresses the beginning of the human age. The rays of lights that came off the Sun, in order to become humans, begin their journey right here, in the $4^{th}$ gate, so that they can enter the Earth and transform into souls in the auric field of the 8 planets in the system. As we know, the number 4 expresses a significant event in the story of the human. The human cycle is possible through the trilogy Mother-Father-Child. Human seed precesses in the penis and preserved here until it is initiated into the womb. Sigmund Freud declared that the penis, which is the transmitter, corresponds to the number 3 (3°) in the unconsciousness. Gemini, which is the first sign that describes the human in the Zodiac, is the third sign. Cancer, which is the sign that secures the reproduction process of humans, is the 4$^{th}$ sign. We should not overlook this information; because the information about ourselves, our reality and our existence live in the unconsciousness. And we can access the information by following such clues.

Humans are a transformed part of the Sun that reflects from the Sun onto the Earth. ***Human spirit is a record written with the Sun light.*** Human existence finds itself in the Sun (in its source.) We know that we should continue reproduction physically so that Earth can stay in its center. The continuation of Earth's incarnation process enables the continuation of other stars' incarnation processes. That is why more physical bodies are needed. Therefore, 4$^{th}$ gate is very essential for our Earth. The Sunlight enters through this gate, incarnates and the same body goes out through this gate. Because 3° is the 4$^{th}$ gate of a house. Enter through the 3°, exit through 4th Gate: the precession of the physical body takes place between two sides of this single gate. And this gate is permanently active.

### 5th GATE:

4° is the 5$^{th}$ gate of a house. It is the gate where Mars transfers the past. Mars descends into the past memories through the 5$^{th}$ gate and rises to the present through the same passage. Mars is the action of our system (not our universe). Transformation cannot emerge without the start of an action. The first action in the creation of the karma always comes before Mars. 4° is always an inward oriented action.

Mars is usually known to be lacking in spirituality. Yet, taking a closer look will show that the case is not so. Mars has an interesting energy. The other face of Mars emerges out of the connection it has with the "Land of the Dead". 4° is activated when Mars is in retrograde. 5$^{th}$ gate is opened widely, which Mars enters and runs towards the very first moments of all the memories you had created in the past. Its purpose is to connect your actions in your past lives with the "first moment" of their creation. Because any relation with everything that moves begins at that moment. Relationship means creating memories. What I mean by relationship here is not about social interactions. It can rather be explained as the relation between two hands that emerges out of the first contact. The energy that flows between lives is the first contact within the process of creating those memories. Mars is not concerned with the content of your memories. It tries to focus on the first moment of the memories. Mars is not aggressive or angry in the "Land of the Dead".

*Let us now understand Mars's mission of initiating life:*

Mars is a perfect guide to help you re-write what has been started in the past when necessary. It is an excellent mentor. It descends into the *End of the Earth* as the Mars that acts in a Scorpion scenario and rises on Earth as the Mars that is ready to act in an Aries scenario. You can imagine Mars in the following way to better understand the "Mars in the Land of the Dead".

The retrograde Mars enters in and runs to the first moments of your past life memories. It awakens the first memory for you. Thus, since retrograde Mars remembers the memory, you and any other elements in nature that are connected to that memory awaken and begin to remember that particular memory. Therefore, during the Mars retrograde period, life frequently shows you signs of remembrance from both your inner or outer worlds. The main message of the unique and incredible courage of the retrograde Mars is as follows: "You have a part in writing the destiny and it is also in your hands to change it. I open the first moment and give you an opportunity. Come back and think. Rewrite your memory. It is totally in your hands to change the past and rewrite it." What else could be the message of the retrograde Mars? This is a noble situation that gives you chances. And this opportunity is presented to us only during the retrograde period of Mars.

*Let us recognize the main message of the retrograde Mars once again:*

"Go to that 'first moment' and rewrite the memories of the past. The present will change when the past is changed. So your future will present a different scenario." This power should be used wisely. It is essential to honor Mars, just like honoring all the other planets. Therefore health, peace and joy will prevail. If you act with the unique courage of the retrograde Mars when 4° is activated, Mars will go through the 5$^{th}$ gate and initiate the healing with respect to the themes of 5$^{th}$ house. The karmic reasons emerge in our personal lives in the areas of love, sexuality, children etc. A liberated person who follows the retrograde Mars and rewrites his past will always experience significant things regarding a passionate love or his/her own child. For example, a person who experiences a misfortunate love life might actually be going through the reflections of his past life memories. If that is the case, things might become smoother for him in these specific matters once he works on this particular exercise.

Retrograde Mars provides us an extraordinary chance so that healthy bodies with healthy minds can be born. That is exactly what Mars is doing each time it begins its retrograde motion. However, *as humans, we are not really aware that planets have retrograde periods so that we can remember our karmic memories, rewrite our time corridors, purify ourselves and evolve.* With the help of this book, we have a wonderful chance to realize this blessing and help them in their work. We can now intentionally help the planets in their work. Retrograde Mars always opened the "first moment" of your karma by going back to past, even though you were not aware of it. And you probably went through unexpected experiences and thought "It is natural to experience these during a retrograde Mars period." Some of you learn life lessons through these experiences, change your attitude or choices and continue your life in a smoother way. Yet you have never realized that you naturally used the chance of rewriting your karma (your own time). You now know what you are achieving. Therefore, I invite you to consciously take part in this special period, which will boost your life energy.

5th gate is not activated at all times. 4° activates when Mars is retrograde. 5th gate opens completely. Mars enters from there and takes all the memories you created in the past and brings them back to Earth. Moreover, when Mars is in retrograde, and under the effect of a transit, its activation continues more intensely until the retrograde period is over. When the effect is over, it closes until a next influence.

### 6th GATE:

5° is the $6^{th}$ gate of a house. It is Jupiter's gate that opens into the past. Jupiter descends into the past memories through the 6th gate and rises to the "present" using the same passage. Jupiter must go into its retrograde period to go into the past memories, just like it is the case for any other planets that naturally enter through the karma gates during the retrograde period. The sign and house of the Jupiter describes the scenario of the past life memories that Jupiter will visit. Faith, relationship with religion and the karma created with distant cultures begin to awaken. These memories are stimulated through Jupiter's light and they are transmitted to the present time in Jupiter's light. Such memories create the duality of health-disease in this life. This is what is reflected through the $6^{th}$ gate.

Venus, Saturn and Jupiter function as channels of knowledge for those leaders who initiate the required knowledge. In this way, when the right time comes, any knowledge that is required by the humanity and Earth is initiated into our space of life and honor us. These 3 planets are channels of knowledge in their own right. In its memory, Jupiter has a passion that encourages humanity for abundance and humaneness. Jupiter takes you to what you are searching for, which is actually nothing but your own self. It brings you insights regarding the conscience and integrity. It reminds you the existence and *rights* of others. Jupiter highlights compassion. It shows that these are the very dynamics that establish your physical health. If Jupiter did not transmit its memory into Pluto in each of its retrograde period, the birth process of our physical bodies would not be the way it is now. This is a crucial information. Your physical form and health depend on the memory that is transferred to Pluto from the 5° of Jupiter.

Having a well-functioning Jupiter might signify a birth with a healthy body. There is a strong correlation between the gradual enhancement of Jupiter's activation each year and the increase in human longevity. It would be impossible for us to transform into physical bodies if there were no Jupiter retrograde periods. Jupiter is not the significator of health or the primordial time, but it has the leading role in directing the initiation of the primordial time and the body into one another. The energy that flows from the 5$^{th}$ degree enables the continuation of this cycle in a regular manner. This is the memory that awakens during the retrograde Jupiter period. It starts a music with the lights of the other planets that brings harmony to all the disorder. By this means our bodies update their health. ***Retrograde movement, by nature, do not break things. It rather exists to purify what begins to degenerate, put things back on track, harmonize the music of the world and correct the orchestra that begins to play in wrong tunes.***

The 6th gate is not always active. 5° activates when Jupiter is retrograde. The 6th gate opens completely. Jupiter enters there and takes all the memories you have created in the past and brings them back on Earth. In addition, when Jupiter receives a transit effect while in retrograde, its activation continues more intensely until the retrograde period is over.

When the effect is over, it closes until a next influence.

### 7th GATE:

6° is the 7th gate of a house. This is where Saturn transfers the past into the present. Saturn descends into the memories through the 7th gate (6°) and rises to the "present" using the same passage. 6° is always the entrance while the 7th gate is the exit for Saturn. I would like to elaborate on Saturn. And this is exactly the right place to do it.

Saturn is the *lord of the first-time corridor* for our system. It is responsible from the "first moment" as well as the beginning and reproduction of time. Saturn should be recognized as the one that possesses the secret of time and prepares the necessary foundation for humans to create time in our system. ***Saturn does not start the time of the humans. It has the knowledge (secret) to unlock the human potential so that humans can create their own time, i.e. so that they can "think". The time of the humans emerges out of the first intentional action of the first human. This is the transformation of intention into "sound" and action. Thoughts create the human time.***

***Time is not single. The characteristics of human time is such that it emerges out of intentional (conscious, deliberate) action. 'The first sound' that starts the time in the universe, which is born out of the first action in that 'first moment' is a humming.*** We know that it is Uranus. Each movement creates a simultaneous 'sound'. ***Sound and movement are actually one and the same.*** Sound, or its following phase, 'music' and movement are one and the same. ***Time begins with music.*** This is true for all the *times* known in our universe. ***The human time emerges out of the combination of sound and thought.*** That is the difference between the human time and a time corridor in the universe. ***Humans cannot continue their incarnation process without "sound", i.e. Music.*** Just like other incarnated forms of matter that need "sound".

That 'first sound' is always the first music. The first music is Uranus. His son Saturn is not music itself however it is subject to the beginning of music and music's state of "being started". Saturn is still subject to the sound that Uranus makes; it can't liberate itself from that sound no matter how much it tries. Nothing can be liberated from the things it emerges out of. It will fail any time it tries. Because nothing dies out once it exists. It is subject to transformation and is in a time corridor now.

***"Once something exists, it can never be 'non-existent'."*** Saturn will forever be a later version of his father, not matter what he does. The total liberation of Saturn from his father would mean that it is not Saturn anymore but a transformed new energy. Children will continue their lives even though their fathers die. They transform into the perfect father in the form of a mental design. Yet, this father in question, which is Uranus, is not mortal. Uranus is an idea. And Saturn is the product of this idea. Saturn is destined to be unable to overcome the father complex.

Time cannot be destroyed. Because thoughts cannot be destroyed. The strongest desire of time is the continuation of 'sound'. ***Continuous and regular production of sound signifies the continuous and regular production of time.*** Saturn desires music and is subject to it, just like others that are subject to the incarnation process.

I underlined that time is the result of the first movement of the first moment, which is music. The mother of time is sound whereas the father of time is moving (movement). The memory that Saturn carries in its light for the beginning of the Earth system, results in the creation of time, i.e. Music. Saturn must be in retrograde motion so that this music is continuous. If Saturn does not go retrograde, music and movement will not be produced in our present lives due to our past life memories. Thoughts will not be possible. Your past memories must create new memories in your present lives and the precession of your daily life should be enhanced in order for time to be born again and again. Your memories are sounds, they rise onto Earth and make you move. Saturn is not the art, the artist, or the music itself; yet if the memory of Saturn was not opened and reflected here in each retrograde period, neither of these concepts would exist in the way they do now. That is why we should understand Saturn very well. *Saturn requires discipline and order; it requires continuous and honest commitment & effort for your objectives. I encourage you to consider these concepts from a profound perspective.* They comprise tremendous power. We manage to create time by overcoming these tests that Saturn continuously teaches us. It is not Saturn but we who creates the human time with the guidance of Saturn. It is we who are the "workers" to create our time. *You will make more and more mistakes unless you stop considering Saturn as a limiting, blocking, or enforcing energy.*

If you comprehend Saturn's memory, you will see that the grand master that teaches you how to travel in time is Saturn. He will teach you how to produce the required energy to travel in time. It is Saturn who owns the sublime energy that will enable you to remember your past karma fully. Mankind should first create his own time to be able to produce memories. *Time is a huge library that is created to store memories.* Time is a memory itself. The greatest memory, *time*, exists because it comprises the memory of humans. ***The "time" you create is the necessary fuel for your other "parts" incarnated in other planets to continue their way.*** Humans that can create their own time have the right to travel in time in their own specific timing. This is what is denoted by the expression "Past, present and future are all in the *moment, now.*" It can be realized by closing two eyes within the moment and turning them inwards. ***Time is a result of human action and humans need time to exist.***

Once *time* becomes a production of humans, it is a living organism that moves independently. Who knows what this energy and memory transforms into, within the universe. The time energy produced at the point might continue to exist as a satellite, dust cloud or asteroid in the orbit of another planet. A particular planet or asteroid might not be able to incarnate or exist at all if we can't produce time. Saturn opens the gate of the time, or memories, that we create. It shows us what we should improve for the good of ourselves and others.

It is Saturn that reminds us time, i.e. our memories. It is the greatest reminder. ***Remembering is traveling through your memories which is traveling in time.*** In retrograde, Saturn transfers the memories of the past through the $7^{th}$ gate. It has *time* itself in its memory and the gate opens completely. Saturn's message is as follows: "If you don't control your own time, you can't integrate with yourself. You will see a stranger each time you look into the mirror, which will give you a sense of unfamiliarity. This inability to integrate with your own self will make you unrestful. And the energy of restlessness will prevent you from being complete and whole within yourself in this incarnation." Think of it this way; just because you fix a disturbing memory in time, you create a partner with whom you will feel complete and whole in this lifetime. You will find out that it is just like fixing the tuning of a musical instrument. Everything will be fine once the tuning is fixed.

Does the time you create support you to feel whole and complete? Does the time act against you or does it work for you? You are the time. Time is nothing but the music that emits from your thoughts and actions.

You can't achieve that perfect inner peace that makes you whole and complete, unless you do not have harmony and accord between different levels of the time. You will always feel lacking. You cannot make yourself complete. This does not necessarily mean that you will meet a partner that makes you feel whole and complete. One should be able to be a partner to herself or himself in a whole and complete manner. This is the most important part.

The 7th gate is not always activated. 6° is activated when Saturn is in retrograde motion. The 7th gate opens completely. Saturn enters there and takes all the memories you have created in the past and brings them back on Earth. In addition, when Saturn receives a transit effect while in retrograde, its activation continues more intensely until the retrograde period is over. When the effect is over, it closes until a next influence.

### 8th GATE:

7° is the 8$^{th}$ gate of a house. This is where Uranus transfers the past into the present. Uranus descends into the past memories through the 7$^{th}$ degree and rises to the "present" using the same passage. 7° is always the entrance into memories while the 8th gate is the exit into life for Uranus. Uranus is responsible from the music itself. It possesses a great energy to be the time itself. It is not Uranus that creates music. Music, i.e. the sound, cannot be created. It is born out of the togetherness of the elements that come together. Uranus is the one that can rule this 'sound'. Sound is not an energy created by a God. ***Death and birth are not created. They are powers that are born out of the togetherness of several different elements. They are manifestations. Death and birth are a unity of power.*** Uranus is responsible of the music that starts the time. It possesses the secret of the sound, the music. It is the ruler of music. Uranus makes itself experienced as Venus on this Earth, as a result of being dismissed from the Earth by Saturn. That is why Venus, the offspring of Uranus, expresses human voice and music on Earth.

The first sound will always be Uranus no matter what Saturn does. For Earth, the sound is always under the control of Venus, which is the earthly version and daughter of Uranus.

Let us now consider the story in the following sequence;
Uranus makes the first sound with the influences coming from different universes, activates others through sound and starts the time in the universe

Saturn starts the time related to our system on Earth

Thoughts start the human time.

Uranus, which is dismissed from the Earth initiates itself as Venus on Earth

Finally, a life cycle begins as a result of the Father-Daughter relationship, on Earth, which is born out of the power struggle between Father & Son

Fathers, their favorable daughters & unfavorable sons.

The great power born out of the relationship between Uranus & Venus is Reincarnation!

Reincarnation is the consciousness, the field, in which the cyclic formation of time corridors can be analyzed. Uranus is amongst us, it lives on Earth. Its name is Venus.

You will read the story in the following pages.

Music expands as soon as the movement begins. Uranus is responsible from the music. Saturn is the "Lord of the Time" for our system. Uranus is the "Lord of the Creation Process of the Time", for the whole universe. He assures that music always flows forward in all the memories. Uranus is responsible of the music that rings in all times. It is the "Lord of Music" that expands to all directions at all times. ***Uranus is a ringing. It is the music of the 'first moment' which is found in the essence of all that is known. It is the sound the sperm makes as it enters the ovaries.*** It is the musical notes of the water flowing from the tap, the first note that rings out as your tears drop from your eyes. The sound you make as you push a door or take a step is under the control of Uranus. It is Uranus that controls the transportation of the memories within the 'sound'. He decides which memory will ring in what time. You will *remember* if Uranus allows you. The activation of memories through certain gates and degrees are determined by the movements of Uranus in the sky. All the lights position themselves according to that main light. It is Uranus who activates the remembering in its general sense and shows where the progress of the activation will end up.

The limits of everything we know, in other words; the point where infinity begins is Pluto. The limit of the limit is Uranus. Uranus is the act of remembering itself. Everything that exists does so in the light of Uranus. We all can exist due to the existence (light and energy) of Uranus. Because it is Venus that gives birth to us. I mentioned that Saturn starts the time in our system; yet the first moment is Uranus. Therefore, "the moment" is Uranus; the first moment of everything is Uranus. ***And time begins with "the moment".*** Saturn, who knows the secret of time for our system and controls it does not actually possess the secret of that first moment. No other gods or goddesses have the secret except Uranus. ***Uranus is the "first moment" about the whole universe.***

*If you perceive Uranus only as a planet, you will drift apart from his nature. Uranus is where we exist. He is not a ring in the reincarnation chain. It is the power in which a ring can exist.* Uranus does not do anything to us. We exist in it. Uranus came into being as a reaction of the relations with the unknown energies in other galaxies. This knowledge is unattainable for us at this point; however, it is certain that the 'first moment' for this galaxy is Uranus.

Uranus is the chord between this galaxy and others. Who knows about the energy of the galaxies that our galaxy is connected to through Uranus. He is the greatest bridge. You might think of Uranus as the python of the galaxy. The presence of Uranus as a reaction rings through its relations with the energies in this galaxy and those of others. It makes 'sound'. This 'sound' hits myriad of things and reacts with them to create music: the musical notes!

This music creates its own karma by ringing and forming the movement. Each karma that is created gets divided into bodies. Ultimately, 'music', the eldest, can form the physical body as a reaction, depending on the characteristics of the relationships it experiences. The musical note *do* (C) materializes as the planet Mars in its incarnation process, as a result of the karma it creates in the universe through its sound and movement. Mars is the physical body of the note *do*. Each concrete object is a physical body and each object had been a sound in the past. All the physical bodies and objects are the result of the karma created by the sound, as a reaction to everything the sound *absorbs* through contact. The greatest power of sound may be hidden in making itself a physical body and object. **Uranus is that very**

***'sound'. The bridge is the 'sound'. And sound is music; bridge is music.***

You can't think of the inexistence of something. It is not possible. Once even a tiny piece of knowledge designed in the mind becomes *known*, it can't be reversed into an unknowable state. Because **Uranus signifies the trace.** And traces cannot be wiped away. Uranus is the energy in which everything exists. You will always come across the 'sound of the first moment' in the mythology of any land you visit. What is universe other than a huge chain of reactions which begins with the 'sound'? All the planets that show themselves and share themselves with us are nothing but the light of Uranus that changes by reacting with different energies. Just like the karma of *do* created Mars as a physical body; *re, mi, fa, sol, la, si* also created their karma and their own physical bodies. Earth's sign is Taurus which represents the Mother Earth. Earth exists through the karma of the sound represented by Venus. It is *C sharp*. Do you now understand why the planet that initiated the karma on our planet manifests itself as Mars? Mars is the physical body of *do*. *Do sharp* is the second tone of the note. The Earth is the physical body of the karma of the *Do* sound. Our planet reaches a very special level in its incarnation process in this period of time.

In this journey, it is able to attract and embody extraordinary sounds that nourish its own intelligence. The Earth might have been designed solely for that purpose. Earth's intelligence is being created every moment based on 4 notes. These are four elements. The 8 planets, 2 lights and Chiron; these 11 different 'sounds' create a tremendous music. This is just like Mozart's playing 11 different 'sounds' at once and making our minds blow. These are the most influential elements in our system. They are the musical symbols of existence. 11 'sounds' give us the clues of the existence.

Try listening to the music according to the elements. Let us now take a closer look at the great reaction that causes 'sound' to be transformed into a physical body. You will receive the knowledge of that incredible music which enables the formation of your physical body.

### *Music according to their elements:*
**Water** RE SHARP, SOL, Sİ (Cancer, Scorpio, Pisces)

**Earth:** DO SHARP (SECOND TONE), FA, LA (Taurus, Virgo, Capricorn)

**Air:** RE, FA SHARP, LA SHARP (Gemini, Libra, Aquarius)

**Fire:** DO, MI, SOL SHARP (Aries, Leo, Sagittarius)

***Music according to signs:***

Aries: DO....Mars; the sound of the first moment for our time corridor

Taurus: DO sharp (SECOND TONE)....Venus; sound of the karma

Gemini: RE....Mercury; sound of the human

Cancer: RE SHARP....Moon; sound of the human heart

Leo: MI....Sun; sound of the spirit

Virgo: FA....Mercury; sound of the plants

Libra: FA SHARP....Venus; sound of the conscience

Scorpio: SOL....Mars and Pluto; the sound of the threshold of the *End of the Earth*, the sound of the ending of the limits

Sagittarius: SOL SHARP....Jupiter; sound of the activation of the dream

Capricorn: LA....Saturn; sound of all the time corridors

Aquarius: LA SHARP....Saturn and Uranus; sound of the sky

Pisces: SÍ....Jupiter and Neptune; sound of the threshold of the End of the Universe

It is interesting to note that the music is positioned in your body in the following way:

*1. chakra: Mars, Do*

*2. chakra: Venus, Re*

*3. chakra: Sun, Mi*

*4. chakra: Moon, Fa*

*5. chakra: Mercury, Sol*

6. chakra: *Jupiter, La*
7. chakra: *Saturn, Si*

## 9th GATE:

8° is the 9$^{th}$ gate of a house. This is where Neptune transfers the past into the present. Neptune descends into the past memories through the 8° and rises to the "present" using the same passage.

What does Neptune carry in its memory? Neptune has the knowledge of infinity. It is related with the end of the galaxy (center). Neptune knows the serenity and coolness as well as a stern nature; it knows how to be connected to the end (heart, center, emptiness) of anything. Not only does Neptune know the memory of the Neptunian activity of humans, but it also has the knowledge and power of connecting the centers (ends) of anything except humans, such as plants, animals etc. Neptune 8° will always open you to infinity. It is metabolized (digestion), it signifies transformation.

It is not sufficient to define transformation within the limits of Plutonian nature. Transformation is the work of Neptune as well. Yet it is not in the form of transforming physical bodies or material; it is Pluto's wisdom. Neptune signifies the wisdom of the total transformation of beings in all of their bodies, namely physical, etheric, astral and self, and the wisdom of the direct communication between the bodies. Neptune is about the integration of the bodies and their reincarnation through transformation. Neptune has the knowledge of the power that incarnates a being with all his/her dimensions. And it is responsible of that process. That is why you read Neptune's energy through the 9$^{th}$ gate, which is the 8$^{th}$ degree.

Pluto, Neptune and Uranus receive memories from the Moon at each New Moon phase. Pluto is the energy field for the physical body to transform in the present time. The information it receives is related to his theme. From the Moon, Neptune receives the memory that serves for the incarnation of all. Since Uranus is the bridge between galaxies, it transfers the memory here into other galaxies and enables our existence. This can be regarded as parallel universes. You now that any information (time, memory) that emerges out of intentional actions are now incarnated in other galaxies through Uranus, do you not? Your actions do not just disappear. They turn into new beings. Just like us, they exist as sources of energies through the power we create. ***Human thought is the "creator" of another galaxy and since it holds the secret of the knowledge of this energy, it transforms into a divine energy in that galaxy.***

**10th GATE:**
9° is the 10th gate of a house. This is where Pluto transfers the past into the present. Pluto descends into the past memories through the 9° and rises to the "present" using the same passage.

*9° has a difference. Each degree is a field that past energies channel themselves through so that they can find their response (return) in this incarnation. Yet 9° has a different mission. It has a role to remind us what is neutralized. Neutralization does not mean the disappearance or ceasing of an energy. Neutralization expresses the change of a created energy as a result of a fundamental transformation.* Any karmic memory that consists of duality itself is transferred to Pluto's memory by Moon and other planets. Then they are transformed to be transferred to other relevant areas. This transformed energy also comes back to you (the person, the space etc. that created the karma). The transformed energy comes into your life through the 9°, which is the 10$^{th}$ gate. Let us assume that you harmed someone in a past life. And this manifests as a health problem in your body in this lifetime. You choose to remember your past life and try to change and neutralize the nature of the negative event by practicing the relevant meditations. This change will not cancel the memory, it rather transforms the memory into something else. ***The purpose here is to transform the negative memory into a positive one that will serve you. Once you practice the transformative work, you will understand the negative memory, as well as the nature of the friendly memory into which it transforms, by following the 9° of a sign.***

Let's assume that a memory that creates a health problem is transferred into this lifetime through the degree of the sign in the $6^{th}$ house of the chart. While you are trying to transform the memory, you have the chance to observe the efficiency of your practice by checking it every month. Once in every month, Moon passes through your $6^{th}$ sign, the Pluto gate which is the 9° and conjuncts the 9°. You should observe your psychological state on that day. Do you feel an inner peace? Do you feel more peaceful and comfortable with the help of the exercises you do, despite the effects of the conjunction? Why? Because Moon conjuncts the 9° of the $6^{th}$ sign once in each month and transfers the transformed memories of the past into your current lifetime.

## 0°-29° Gates

### Exemplary Reading:
*1st Decan*

0° Cancer, 1st Gate of the 1st Decan; Moon is the 1st Gate (Moon at 0° is always the 1st Gate of the 1st Decan)

1° Cancer, 2nd Gate of the 1st Decan; Mercury is the 2nd Gate (Mercury at 1° is always the 2nd Gate of the 1st Decan)

2° Cancer, 3rd Gate of the 1st Decan; Venus is the 3rd Gate (Venus at 2° is always the 3rd Gate of the 1st Decan)

3° Cancer, 4th Gate of the 1st Decan; Sun is the 4th Gate. (Sun at 3° is always the 4th Gate of the 1st Decan)

4° Cancer, 5th Gate of the 1st Decan; Mars is the 5th Gate. (Mars at 4° is always the 5th Gate of the 1st Decan)

5°Cancer, 6th Gate of the 1st Decan; Jupiter is the 6th Gate (Jupiter at 5° is always the 6th Gate of the 1st Decan)

6° Cancer, 7th Gate of the 1st Decan; Saturn is the 7th Gate (Saturn at 6° is always the 7th Gate of the 1st Decan)

7° Cancer, 8th Gate of the 1st Decan; Uranus is the 8th Gate (Uranus at 7° is always the 8th Gate of the 1st Decan)

8° Cancer, 9th Gate of the 1st Decan; Neptune is the 9th Gate (Neptune at 8° is always the 9th Gate of the 1st Decan)

9° Cancer, 10th Gate of the 1st Decan; Pluto is the 10th Gate (Pluto at 9° is always the 10th Gate of the 1st Decan)

**Exemplary reading from 10° onwards;**
9s are subtracted from each high degree.

*10°= 10-9= 1st gate, 0° Moon.*
*11°= 11-9= 2nd gate, 1° Mercury.*
*12°=12-9= 3rd gate, 2° Venus.*

Or you can read each degree separately as follows.

Let's assume that the cusp of a house in the natal chart is 10° Cancer.

### *2nd Decan*

*10° Cancer, 1st Gate of the 2nd Decan; Moon is the 1st Gate. (The Moon at 10° is always the 1st Gate of the 2nd Decan.)*

*11° Cancer, 2nd Gate of the 2nd Decan; Mercury is the 2nd Gate. (Mercury at 11° is always the 2nd Gate of the 2nd Decan.)*

*12° Cancer, 3rd Gate of the 2nd Decan; Venus is the 3rd Gate. (Venus at 12° is always the 3rd Gate of the 2nd Decan.)*

*13° Cancer, 4th Gate of the 2nd Decan; Sun is the 4th Gate. (The Sun at 13° is always the 4th Gate of the 2nd Decan.)*

*14° Cancer, 5th Gate of the 2nd Decan; Mars is the 5th Gate. (Mars at 14° is always the 5th Gate of the 2nd Decan.)*

*15° Cancer sign, 6th Gate of the 2nd Decan; Jupiter is the 6th Gate. (Jupiter at 15° is always the 6th Gate of the 2nd Decan.)*

*16° Cancer, 7th Gate of the 2nd Decan; Saturn is the 7th Gate. (Saturn at 16 ° is always the 7th Gate of the 2nd Decan.)*

*17° Cancer, 8th Gate of the 2nd Decan; Uranus is the 8th Gate. (Uranus at 17° is always the 8th Gate of the 2nd Decan.)*

*18 ° Cancer, 9th Gate of the 2nd Decan; Neptune is the 9th Gate. (Neptune at 18° is always the 9th Gate of the 2nd Decan.)*

*19 ° Cancer sign, 10th Gate of the 2nd Decan; Pluto is the 10th Gate. (Pluto at 19° is always the 10th Gate of the 2nd Decan.)*

### 3rd Decan

*20° Cancer, 1st Gate of the 3rd Decan; Moon is the 1st Gate. (Moon at 20 ° is always the 1st Gate of the 3rd Decan.)*

*21° Cancer, 2nd Gate of the 3rd Decan; Mercury is the 2nd Gate. (Mercury at 21 ° is always the 2nd Gate of the 3rd Decan.)*

*22° Cancer, 3rd Gate of the 3rd Decan; Venus is the 3rd Gate. (Venus at 22 ° is always the 3rd Gate of the 3rd Decan.)*

*23° Cancer, 4th Gate of the 3rd Decan; Sun is the 4th Gate. (Sun at 23 ° is always the 4th Gate of the 3rd Decan.)*

*24° Cancer, 5th Gate of the 3rd Decan; Mars is the 5th Gate. (Mars at 24 ° is always the 5th Gate of the 3rd Decan.)*

*25° Cancer, 6th Gate of the 3rd Decan; Jupiter is the 6th Gate. (Jupiter at 25 ° is always the 6th Gate of the 3rd Decan.)*

*26° Cancer, 7th Gate of the 3rd Decan; Saturn is the 7th Gate. (Saturn at 26 ° is always the 7th Gate of the 3rd Decan.)*

*27° Cancer, 8th Gate of the 3rd Decan; Uranus is the 8th Gate. (Uranus at 27 ° is always the 8th Gate of the 3rd Decan.)*

*28 ° Cancer, the 9th Gate of the 3rd Decan; Neptune is the 9th Gate. (Neptune at 28 ° is always the 9th Gate of the 3rd Decan.)*

*29 ° Cancer, 10th Gate of the 3rd Decan; Pluto is the 10th Gate. (Pluto at 29 ° is always the 10th Gate of the 3rd Decan.)*

### Main Gate:

Remembering the past lives begins when the 9°of a particular sign is activated. The gate of remembering is opened when the related planet is in its retrograde motion and makes an aspect to the 9°of the sign or when Moon conjuncts the 9° of the that sign. Therefore the house is completely activated and awakened. The 9° represented by Pluto, which is the time corridor that opens into the *End of the Earth*, is activated. This is also the 10$^{th}$ gate of that particular sign.

This gate belongs to Pluto. To remember the past lives in a chart, you should begin to track with the 9°of a particular sign and follow the 10°, 11°, 12°, 13°, 14°, 15°, 16°, 17°, 18°, 19°, 20°, 21°, 22°, 23°, 24°, 25°, 26°, 27°, 28°, 29°. For example; let us assume that the native cannot find what he is looking for in love. He experiences the weirdest experiences in his private life.

His Hermetic Astrologer will be the right person to tell him if this situation arises from the past lives or not. It is crucial that the Hermetic Astrologer tells the native about his shadow side or trauma. He should tell the house and planet (with its sign) that transfer this shadow/trauma into the current lifetime. Which house is that? And what is the sign of the house? Which planet is it that transfers the shadow into this lifetime? Let's assume that the Hermetic astrologer sees that Libra is the sign that describes love in the natal chart. And he finds out when Mercury, which transmits the trauma of the past life, will make an aspect to the 9° Libra when it is in the retrograde motion. Mercury makes its retrograde motion in Libra in long time intervals.

If the native prefers the exercises right ahead, he can follow the daily movements of Moon. Is the native chooses to remember that particular lifetime to solve the problem, we should tell him: "We will follow the transiting Moon. Your trauma comes through Libra into this life and characterizes Libra themes. We will wait patiently for the Moon in Libra to reach 9°." The moment Moon conjuncts the 9° Libra, the time corridor that opens into the *End of the Earth,* which is represented by Pluto, is activated. Thus, the whole axis starts to be activated and awakened. Now is the right time to begin the remembering exercises. The exercises are in the following.

*Let us now understand the harmony of the 9° in the houses.*

Let's count the first 9 degrees of a house;
0°, 1°, 2°, 3°, 4°, 5°, 6°, 7°, 8°, which are 9 in number.
The sum is 36° and note that 3+6=9.

There is an interesting harmony here. These 9 degrees are respectively; Moon (0°) - Mercury (1°) - Venus (2°) - Sun (3°) - Mars (4°) - Jupiter (5°) - Saturn (6°) - Uranus (7°) - Neptune (8°) - Pluto (9°)' dur. The knowledge in its pure form directly awakens from those fields represented by these degrees. In this way, Moon opens the past life gates. The past karma begins to flow "here", which means it gets activated in this lifetime.

This activation is a chance. You might ask "Didn't you just mention that remembering begins when the retrograde planet makes an aspect to the 9°of a sign?" Yes, that is true. Yet there is more to it; Moon already attracts the information of the degrees between 0-8 in any sign it enters during the 7 phases after the New Moon. Through this readiness, it can finally awaken the memories when it arrives at the 9°. It can activate the time corridor that goes to Pluto with this power. When Moon reaches the New Moon phase and begins its unique retrograde motion, the foundation which will transfer the information to Pluto is ready. The memories of the past lives are welcomed into our lives through the degrees activated by the Moon. We just need to grasp these "ghostly energies" and transform them into friendly ones.

Let us remember that the Moon absorbs any memory we create at any moment and acts to transfer those memories to the *threshold of the End of the Earth* in New Moon phase. If we succeed in transforming these 'ghostly energies' into friendly energies, the Moon will easily makes us notice whether we are at peace with this energy or not in the next month. For example; when the Moon enters into a sign of our natal chart and opens the gates the next month, the energy of the karmic memory with which we reconciled in our meditations will this time reflects on us as positive karma. This time, it might bring us great experiences. Because the memory that represented that trauma has now transformed into a peaceful memory that supports and satisfies us. It does not sabotage us anymore. We might describe it as "changing one's past life scenario". These karmic memories should first be evoked by the nature so that they can be transformed. Moon is the first to takes on this duty.

*Some more information about the exercises:*

The energy of healing is active after the 9°. Moon will respectively conjunct 10°, 11°, 12°, 13°, 14°, 15°, 16°, 17°, 18°, 19°, 20°, 21°, 22°, 23°, 24°, 25°, 26°, 27°, 28°, 29°. This is an important point for your daily exercises. Because you will be practicing the meditation in the very hour of the conjunction when Moon conjuncts a particular degree. The exercises are based on the activation of the degrees. Each degree becomes functional through the rulership of the related planet, so you need to practice the meditation for the planets. I call them ***Meditation of the Nines***.

***Meditation of the Nines: Mercury, Venus, Sun, Mars, Jupiter, Saturn, Uranus, Neptune, Pluto***

These are the meditations to realize, in a controlled way, the information awakened for the 30 gates between 0°-29° and easily neutralize them by transforming them into friendly energies. It is a must to practice these meditations in the right time in order to transform the memories. So when is the right time? When Moon comes on the 9° of that house, we begin the exercises for that month starting with that of the 9°. Then we do the specific meditation at each degree Moon makes a conjunction with and complete the process with the 29°. The information for the practice of the 30 gates between 0°-29° is as follows:

### *For the 1st Decan*

***1st Gate:*** *For Moon at 0° - When Moon conjunct 0° of that sign, you will do the Moon meditation.*
***2nd Gate:*** *For Mercury at 1° - When Moon conjunct 1° of that sign, you will do the Mercury meditation.*
***3rd Gate:*** *For Venus at 2° - When Moon conjunct 2° of that sign, you will do the Venus meditation.*
***4th Gate:*** *For Sun at 3° - When Moon conjunct 3° of that sign, you will do the Sun meditation.*
***5th Gate:*** *For Mars at 4° - When Moon conjunct 4° of that sign, you will do the Mars meditation.*
***6th Gate:*** *For Jupiter at 5° - When Moon conjunct 5° of that sign, you will do the Jupiter meditation.*
***7th Gate:*** *For Saturn at 6° - When Moon conjunct 6° of that sign, you will do the Saturn meditation.*
***8th Gate:*** *For Uranus at 7° - When Moon conjunct 7° of that sign, you will do the Uranus meditation.*
***9th Gate:*** *For Neptune at 8° - When Moon conjunct 8° of that sign, you will do the Neptune meditation.*

**10th Gate:** *For Pluto at 9° - When Moon conjunct 9° of that sign, you will do the Pluto meditation.*

### *For the 2nd Decan*

**11th Gate:** *For Moon at 10° - When Moon conjunct 10° of that sign, you will do the Moon meditation.*

**12th Gate:** *For Mercury at 11° - When Moon conjunct 11° of that sign, you will do the Mercury meditation.*

**13th Gate:** *For Venus at 12° - When Moon conjunct 12° of that sign, you will do the Venus meditation.*

**14th Gate:** *For Sun at 13° - When Moon conjunct 13° of that sign, you will do the Sun meditation.*

**15th Gate:** *For Mars at 14° - When Moon conjunct 14° of that sign, you will do the Mars meditation.*

**16th Gate:** *For Jupiter at 15° - When Moon conjunct 15° of that sign, you will do the Jupiter meditation.*

**17th Gate:** *For Saturn at 16° - When Moon conjunct 16° of that sign, you will do the Saturn meditation.*

**18th Gate:** *For Uranus at 17° - When Moon conjunct 17° of that sign, you will do the Uranus meditation.*

**19th Gate:** *For Neptune at 18° - When Moon conjunct 18° of that sign, you will do the Neptune meditation.*

**20th Gate:** *For Pluto at 19° - When Moon conjunct 19° of that sign, you will do the Pluto meditation.*

### For the 3rd Decan

**21st Gate:** *For Moon at 20° - When Moon conjunct 20° of that sign, you will do the Moon meditation.*

**22nd Gate:** *For Mercury at 21° - When Moon conjunct 21° of that sign, you will do the Mercury meditation.*

**23rd Gate:** *For Venus at 22° - When Moon conjunct 22° of that sign, you will do the Venus meditation.*

**24th Gate:** *For Sun at 23° - When Moon conjunct 23° of that sign, you will do the Sun meditation.*

**25th Gate:** *For Mars at 24° - When Moon conjunct 24° of that sign, you will do the Mars meditation.*

**26th Gate:** *For Jupiter at 25° - When Moon conjunct 25° of that sign, you will do the Jupiter meditation.*

**27th Gate:** *For Saturn at 26° - When Moon conjunct 26° of that sign, you will do the Saturn meditation.*

**28th Gate:** *For Uranus at 27° - When Moon conjunct 27° of that sign, you will do the Uranus meditation.*

**29th Gate:** *For Neptune at 28° - When Moon conjunct 28° of that sign, you will do the Neptune meditation.*

**30th Gate:** *For Pluto at 29° - When Moon conjunct 29° of that sign, you will do the Pluto meditation.*

Moon opens the memory of the past lives and welcomes when it enters the 0°-8° of a sign but the information cannot be activated in a meaningful way yet at this phase. For that activation, Moon should touch the 9° of the sign it is found in. When the Plutonic energy of the *End of the Earth* activates, we can begin transforming the memories into friendly energies through the meditations. When Moon completes its conjunction with the 29° of the sign it is found in, the exercises of remembering and transforming for that sign are completed as well. And we say "the karmic memories of that sign is transformed". The next month, when Moon activates 9° of that sign through the power of the karmic memory it derives from the 0°- 8°, it becomes easier for us to observe how much renewal has occurred in the issues of that axis.

## Memories Activated in Decanates

1st Decanate comprises the gates of personal karmic memories.

2nd Decanate comprises the gates of the collective karma of the planet.

3rd Decanate comprises the gates of the universe's memories.

A planet that retrogrades at 0 °, 1 °, 2 °, 3 °, 4 °, 5 °, 6 °, 7 °, 8 °, 9° directs its personal karmic memory regarding that specific matter towards our planet.

A planet that retrogrades at 10 °, 11 °, 12 °, 13 °, 14 °, 15 °, 16 °, 17 °, 18 °, 19° directs the memory of the karma between the planet and the collective, regarding that specific matter, towards our planet.

A planet that retrogrades at 29 °, 28 °, 27 °, 26 °, 25 °, 24 °, 23 °, 22 °, 21 °, 20° directs the memory of the universe regarding that specific matter towards our planet.

Let's assume that retrograde Mercury is at the 27° in Scorpio. Since 27° represent the Uranus memory (it is also the exaltation degree of Venus), that means Uranus memory is active and in communication with the planet. We are exposed to the information of that memory and it is exposed to our information as well. We are informed about one another in this way.

## Moon Meditation and Meditation of the Nines

### Moon Meditation

The 0° of a sign is its first degree. It is ruled by the pure Moon light. Rather than creating karma, this degree represents the entrance of a specific Moon into the human system. This is a Moon that is getting ready to record into its chakras the actions which will be realized with intention. That is why it is better to honor the

Moon that enters into our system through the 0° by remembering the 4th chakra which is emphasized by the Moon. Heart is the end of humans. It is perfect for a human to begin the exercises by connecting with the threshold of his own end. Your heart chakra is such a threshold that one step further of it is timelessness. And a step before that threshold is life itself. This is the threshold of your being. It might be described as a conscious communication with the Moon.

Meditation is simple.

*Name: Moon Meditation for 0°*
*Time: 20 minutes at least*
*Place: You should be alone in a silent place with no music*
*Exercise:*

*Sit down and close your eyes. Relax as you slow down your breathing. Breathe in and out through your heart chakra. Just feel yourself in your heart chakra. Feel that you are transformed into silence and space itself. Transform into emptiness. There will be a natural rhythm after a while. Here is a tip to understand if your meditation is effective; you will feel a great pleasure in your heart chakra each time you breathe in and out. The longer you extend the duration of this meditation, the more spectacular results you will get.*

*Name: Mercury Meditation for 1°*
*Time: 20 minutes at least*

*Place:* You should be alone in a silent place with no music
*Exercise:*

*Begin by doing the moon meditation. Once you begin to experience the pleasure in your heart chakra, direct the energy of the pure light in your Moon chakra into your throat chakra (fifth chakra). Feel the energy intensifying there. You might cough or swallow. It is natural and temporal. Feel the connection between your heart and throat chakra deeply and enjoy it. As soon as your meditation is over, write down in your meditation log, which should keep near, any symbol, memory, number, sound etc. that might have been triggered during the meditation.*

*Name: Venus Meditation for 2°*
*Time: 20 minutes at least*
*Place: You should be alone in a silent place with no music*
*Exercise:*

*Begin by doing the Moon meditation. Once you begin to experience the pleasure in your heart chakra, direct the energy of the pure light in your Moon chakra into your second chakra. Feel the energy intensifying there. Allow yourself to be fascinated by the pure energies of Moon and Venus and feel the pleasure. Stay with your breath, without thinking anything. Remember! And continue your meditation feeling the satisfaction of being transformed into the emptiness and space itself. As soon as your meditation is over, write down in your meditation log any symbol, memory, number, sound etc. that might have been triggered during the meditation.*

*Name: Sun Meditation for 3°*
*Time: 20 minutes at least*
*Place: You should be alone in a silent place with no music*
*Exercise:*

*Begin by doing the Moon meditation. Once you begin to experience the pleasure in your heart chakra, direct the energy of the pure light in your Moon chakra into your third chakra. Feel the energy intensifying there. It is natural to feel sensitive in your stomach and abdominal area. Continue until you feel a slight weight on your navel. Enjoy this wonderful convergence of lights. Feel the great pleasure wrapping your body. As soon as your meditation is over, write down in your meditation log any symbol, memory, number, sound etc. that might have been triggered during the meditation.*

*Name: Mars Meditation for 4°*
*Time: 20 minutes at least*
*Place: You should be alone in a silent place with no music*
*Exercise:*

*Begin by doing the Moon meditation. Once you begin to experience the pleasure in your heart chakra, direct the energy of the pure light in your Moon chakra into your root chakra. Feel the energy intensifying there.*

*Experience how this energy empowers your root chakra and intensifies the flow of energy there. Continue until the focus feels more powerful. Observe how that great pleasure spreading from your heart nourishes and embraces your root chakra. As soon as your meditation is over, write down in your meditation log any symbol, memory, number, sound etc. that might have been triggered during the meditation.*

>Name: Jupiter Meditation for 5°
>Time: 20 minutes at least
>Place: You should be alone in a silent place with no music
>Exercise:

*Begin by doing the Moon meditation. Once you begin to experience the pleasure in your heart chakra, direct the energy of the pure light in your Moon chakra into your sixth chakra (your third eye). Feel the energy intensifying there. You will feel a focus point, a slight weight on your forehead. It will give you a feeling of peace to unite the pleasure in your heart chakra and the pure energy of your third eye. You will feel a great pleasure as you experience the energy expanding in your head as if dancing. Let yourself feel the splendid feeling of pleasure. As soon as your meditation is over, write down in your meditation log any symbol, memory, number, sound etc. that might have been triggered during the meditation.*

>Name: Saturn Meditation for 6°
>Time: 20 minutes at least

*Place: You should be alone in a silent place with no music*
*Exercise:*

*Begin by doing the Moon meditation. Once you begin to experience the pleasure in your heart chakra, direct the energy of the pure light in your Moon chakra into your seventh chakra (right above your head). Feel the energy intensifying there. You will feel a slight pressure on your head. You will feel as if nymphs are dancing on your crown chakra. It is a wonderful union of energies. It will make you feel as if you are physically attached to somewhere. You will feel the pleasure of being connected. Enjoy it. As soon as your meditation is over, write down in your meditation log any symbol, memory, number, sound etc. that might have been triggered during the meditation.*

*Name: Uranus Meditation for 7°*
*Time: 20 minutes at least*
*Place: You should be alone in a silent place with no music*
*Exercise:*

*Begin by doing the Moon meditation. Once you begin to experience the pleasure in your heart chakra, expand the energy of the pure light in your Moon chakra into the universe and throughout your body. Feel that you are embracing everything with this pure moon light. You will feel that there is a power that provides your connection in every particle of the universe and you never realized it before. It will give you a tremendous power* which is almost impossible to describe. You will feel an incredible sense of satisfaction everywhere. Enjoy it. As soon as your meditation is over, write down in your meditation log any symbol, memory, number, sound etc. that might have been triggered during the meditation.

>Name: Neptune Meditation for 8°
>Time: 20 minutes at least
>Place: You should be alone in a silent place with

no music

>Exercise:

Begin by doing the Moon meditation. Once you begin to experience the pleasure in your heart chakra, direct the energy of the pure light in your Moon chakra to connect with that spot in the universe where you feel you really belong to. How will you know that you are really experiencing the pleasure? You will notice a pulse right on your head. This is a magical moment of connecting with the inspiration itself which is found everywhere in the universe. The heart of the universe will be perfectly in tune with you and you will be dancing within the music of the universe. Enjoy this wonderful experience. As soon as your meditation is over, write down in your meditation log any symbol, memory, number, sound etc. that might have been triggered during the meditation.

>Name: Pluto Meditation for 9°
>Time: 20 minutes at least
>Place: You should be alone in a silent place with

no music

>Exercise:

*Begin by doing the Moon meditation. Once you begin to experience the pleasure in your heart chakra, direct the energy of the pure light in your Moon chakra to feel a state that will connect you to the end of everything that is ever known. This spot is a threshold between life and no life. It is cold, peaceful, comfortable and easy. It is the end of everything that you know about life, that is all you need to know about this spot. Do not take it as death though. This is an undefined space. Time corridors have not been built here to be transformed into memories yet. It is the most virgin place in the universe. Just initiate yourself into that threshold.*

*You will feel wonderful when you achieve this exercise. It will not be possible to see life as you did before. Why? Because you will witness that life is just something that changes, transforms and flows in every moment. You will realize that you are not the center of the Earth. I call this "awakening to the truth", based on my own experiences. It gives you an extraordinary feeling of pleasure.* **Enjoy awakening to the truth.** *As soon as your meditation is over, write down in your meditation log any symbol, memory, number, sound etc. that might have been triggered during the meditation.*

Here is an example of a *"remembering exercise"*.

I had a client who wanted to remember his past live. I first analyzed his chart to specify his sex in that lifetime and the faculties that might have been incarnated with him into his current lifetime. I began to observe the relation between the transit Moon, which is effective for remembering, and his natal chart. He began the exercises of the degree when Moon began to conjunct the 0° of the related sign. So he did the *meditation of the Nines* for every degree, including the 29°, until the Moon transits are over. Moon opens a gate and activates the information at each degree Moon moves into. I suggested that he uses a meditation log to see the effects of the information that was activated in his life. When Moon triggered the degrees which represented the negative aspects in the natal chart, he could achieve to neutralize each memory that was transferred through the gates by doing the related meditation.

When the Moon transit was finally over, I evaluated his meditation log in a meeting I had with the client. His confidence was reinforced when he saw the consistent and striking results. We decided to follow the Moon transits for the coming month. He began doing the same exercises when Moon came to the 0° of that particular house. And he continued with the exercises until the Moon finished its relation with the sign over the transits. He wrote about his meditations in his log during the process. In the following month, he was in a wonderful mood, feeling satisfied, peaceful, and calm. He said "It feels as if I had left somethings behind. I feel that I had been carrying a heavy burden and I know that I had left it. I am calmer, more peaceful, and happier. It is as if I have made a peace contract with everything. I do not get offended easily, it feels as if a magical wand has touched my vulnerability. That feeling of *I have to fight for living*, was replaced by *I will have whatever I need*. I am so proud of my client. He did a great job. Why? Because he just feels fine now. That's why everything connected with him is also fine.

There was another client I worked with. Due to the dynamics of his chart, we began the process by following the Mercury before and after its retrograde motion. His former life time was deciphered using the method of Hermetic Astrology. I learnt about the life field that his past life traumas were connected to, via the help of the planet in the related sign.

Mercury was going to begin its retrograde motion on 18th of November, at 13° Sagittarius, which would last 20 days.

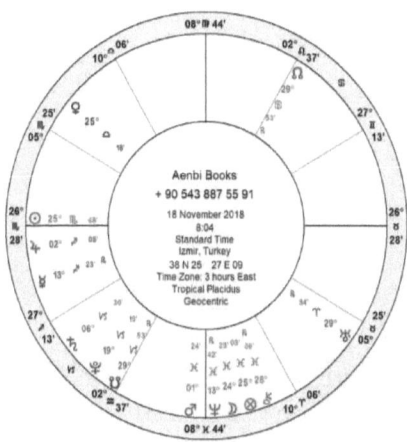

It then would be stationary at 27° in Scorpio and begin its direct motion towards the Sagittarius constellation. I love this situation. Because this is where Mercury, by emitting an energy that seems "retrograde", activates the most hidden memories of the karma at depth to come to surface on Earth. The most important thing to be calculated was how many days before the retrograde Mercury would conjunct the 0° Sagittarius. Based on my calculations, I found that Mercury would arrive 0°Saggitarius on October 31.

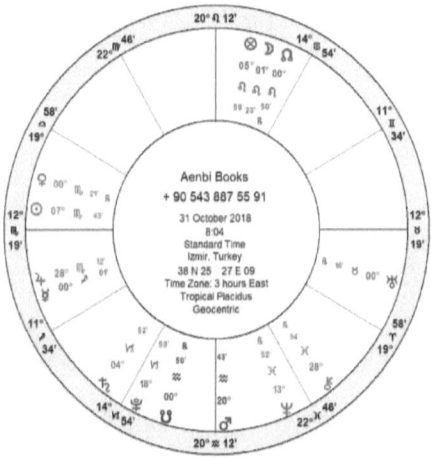

Therefore, he needed to begin the *Meditations of the Nines* on October 31.

The difference of the interpretation regarding the retrograde meditation and that of transit Moon is that here, we know beforehand which memories would be awakened from the client's past. We are aware which memories would come and what they would transform into. We make our plans to rewrite the time and wait for the memories to be revealed. We know what is and will be awakening. *Meditation of the Nines* is applied the same way with a little difference. The difference is that we connect the Mercury chakra to the other two chakras we use, namely the Moon chakra and the chakra of the related planet, in all planetary meditations.

The client began the *Meditation of the Nines* when Mercury was 0° Sagittarius on October 31 and he continued until Mercury began its retrograde movement at 13° Sagittarius on November 18. He did the exercise for 20 minutes every day. Then, he continued to repeat the daily planetary meditations backwards regularly, from the 0° until 13°, by following the Mercury that goes retrograde towards the 12°. Since the retrograde Mercury would complete its retrograde motion in Sagittarius and pass through 29 °, 28 °, 27 ° of the previous sign, which is Scorpio, to complete its stationary period; the client added the planetary meditations of those three degrees in his assignment list.

So what is the retrograde Mercury doing during this time?

Mercury manages to open the gates of the fourteen degrees one by one after it enters Sagittarius, and it can use these gates as a foundation to descend into the *End of the Earth*. Mercury achieves to descend through all the karma gates it has opens until December 7 (including 29°, 28°, 27°of Scorpio. So it makes 17 degrees in total.) and ascend with new karmic songs. It is wonderful to watch the unique dance of Mercury. You can't even imagine the things it can make you experience. This is a music that can only be heard in the depths of a body that has gained sensitivity through the meditations.

Exercises practiced during retrograde periods are very special and deep times of remembering.

*"Human spirit is a record written in the Sunlight."*

**Remember**

*Remember*

*Ahura Sevgi Alis Yıldırım*

# THE STORY OF THE SOUL

There is a romantic story that can be traced back to ancient Egypt. The soul heads to Polaris once it separates from the body and goes towards the other worlds. Although Polaris is interpreted as the energy field through which a soul enters and leaves the Earth, I will focus on another point in my exploration. Because we know that the spirit celestially enters the system only once and where it exists is not through the same place. There is a tremendous library of consciousness hidden in this epic story.

Before taking their physical bodies, our souls take on the related memories from the Moon light and 8 planets, whose incarnations depend on us. Because every soul knows that any time corridor created in our system, which are the past life memories, still reside in the memory of these planets. It is also known by the souls that a soul that is attracted to the magnetic field of the Earth will unite with the strange object called the physical body, as required by the mechanism of duality. That is why anything that has the *number 9* is crucial. These 9 celestial elements are the main power fields souls are connected to, as they re-enter or exit this system of duality. Souls are connected to the same fields as they continue to exist in the system as well. These 9 celestial elements need the memory, i.e. the energy, which will be created by the process of duality so that they can continue with their own incarnations.

Let us be taken by this epic narration and say that, just like the ancient Egyptian priests regarded, our souls have come from beyond the star Polaris and headed towards the duality, where the universe is grounded, to be materialized. The soul cannot come here without first going through the systems of the Moon and the 8 planets and taking on the records of the past life memories. The soul has to pass through the time corridors one by one. Because there are karmic knowledge that the soul needs to take from each library of time. Before coming to Earth, it takes the memory of the galactic system into its aura from each planet it passes through. Yes, the soul has an aura as well. Nevertheless it is not similar to the magnetic fields of the objects. Let us take Venus as an example. What does a soul receive when it 'hits' Venus? It receives the knowledge of the themes represented by Venus, such as love, sexuality, enjoying life, justice, peace etc. The aspects between the planets tell us how much support the soul will receive from this knowledge during its lifetime. What else defines an aspect anyway? Of course, the soul stops by Mars as it takes the memories of those themes from Venus. From Mars, it receives the memory of each knowledge with which the human creates using his actions, any karma that he will do, the moment of the first action as well as the memory of war, fighting, competition and every thoughtless creation. That is how the soul receives knowledge by stopping by at each 9 celestial elements.

Each person is a memory. *Man is a memory that must remember himself.* People want to know who they are and which planet in the sky they represent on Earth. There are essentially 9 memories in you. You are being who exist as a result of the combination of 9 memories. Your incarnation is necessary and obligatory on our Earth, the place where the universe is grounded, with a certain intertwining of the memories of the 9 celestial elements, namely the Moon, Sun and 7 planets. *You each are a cocktail of the 9 celestial elements on this Earth.* Do you perceive yourself as an independent chain of incarnations independent of everything else? You are wrong. You are the incarnated Sun, Moon, Venus, Mars, Mercury, Jupiter, Saturn and Neptune. *The great Nines are you.* Earth is where the universe is grounded.

*A human is an antenna that connects the 9 celestial elements in the sky, each of which is a chakra of the universe, to the Earth.* A human is the connection itself between the universe and Earth. *If the soul cannot transform into a physical body by being "taken" by the duality in this Earth chakra, karma cannot*

***be created.*** In other words, the energy of the power of thought required by the universe cannot become a dynamic (source) of energy production (source). Every karmic energy you create is actually the energy required for each of the 9 celestial elements to be incarnated. ***Humans are the energy centers, the sources of information, that produce the memory necessary for the planets to continue their journey.***

In its incarnation journey, Venus is able to connect itself to Earth, the field where the universe is grounded, through the human body. Thus, the opportunity arises for Venus to materialize itself. Venus is grounded, in other words incarnates, thanks to the Earth just as it is the case with the other 8 celestial elements.

Let me make it clear with a narration.

Think of a meeting room. There is a sage at the entrance. 3 planets apply here. They say; *'We have reached such a level in our incarnation in this galaxy. We don't know what to do next. They said we should come here to you '.*

At that moment, the sage opens the doors of the meeting room, takes these 3 planets in, and begins to train them:

*"You now have the authority to connect to the root chakra of the universe in a direct way and dominate the*

*memory. You have now reached the maturity to have a say in the functioning of the entire universe. In order for you to do this, you will now learn to connect directly with the chakras of the entire universe at this stage of your incarnation. In time, you will transform into chakras, too. It will determine what you will become in your next incarnation once you make this connection. You are now the masters of memory."*

And all of a sudden on a huge movie screen, Our Earth appears with its vivid, magnificently colorful aura.

*"Let me introduce you the root chakra of the universe, through which the universe materializes, grounds and transforms itself. This is the other half of the Sun and its mirror. Its name is Earth. You will need to connect to this chakra to continue your journey from now on. In order to do this, you must have a very good understanding of the functioning there. Before you can enter the root chakra of the universe, all 3 of you must start a collective work together. You all have to unite your own memories. You have to unite your own memories and connect to the root chakra of the universe and nourish yourselves from this source.*

*Think of it like a baby's breast milk. As long as the baby receives this milk, he will be able to continue his way. So why do you need to connect to the root chakra of the universe at this stage of your incarnation? Because the human soul also needs to create its own opposition, i.e. its mirror.* **The opposition of the soul is the body it lives in. The purpose of all the** *planets that have achieved duality is becoming free by transforming into a source of life. That is what Uranus has taught this galaxy.* Here is the main theme of our galaxy: being aware of our coexistence with one another and becoming free sources of energy. This is the fundamental thesis of the establishment of our universe. We are all trying to complete this fundamental thesis. You, the 3 planets; if you want your own duality to begin, which means having your own root chakra, you will be able to learn it by connecting to the root chakra of the universe. For this I give you a pure light from the Sun. Pure light signifies a form of light that has no memory'.

Suddenly, a pure bright light from the Sun appears in the center of the table. And the sage turns to the 3 planets and says: *"What you know best is what you have reached the secrets of and governed during your own incarnations."*

There is Moon in the meeting room as well. Moon is the closest to Earth's root chakra and is the one who knows it most closely. For this reason, it has the secret of being able to see what's ahead and knows how things work during the times of darkness on Earth. Moon guides the 8 planets. Because it was born from the root chakra. Moon is an experienced guide who is well acquainted with the functioning of duality. Moon acts like a translator in Earth's relation with the 8 planets. It knows the language of the Earth well and translates it to other planets so that they can all connect. She is a good translator and a good guide. The Moon loads the pure light with this secret. Mars stretches out his hand and gives his own memory to the light Moon has loaded with the secret. What Mars has learned best so far is the secret of motion. Mars has the secret of initiating creation. It can give this secret. Venus has the secret of creating with love and can give it to others. Mercury has the secret of the creation of what is called thinking and this is what it loads others with. Jupiter, accompanying them in the hall, has the knowledge of how an existing thing transforms into a belief. That is what Jupiter can load. Saturn has the secret of the workings of the memory and it can load others with this secret. Pluto acts as a guide in connecting Venus, Mars and Mercury to Earth so that they can have their own dualities in their own journey of karma. Saturn is the library which is responsible for recording any information produced during the planets' own incarnation processes.

Suddenly, something interesting happens in the hall; Moon, Saturn, Jupiter, Pluto, Uranus and Neptune stand opposite to Venus, Mars and Mercury. They have a smile on their faces. It is as if they will confess their true identity to Venus, Mars, Mercury for the first time. The sage says:

*'We will no longer hide it from you. It's time to reveal the big secret. These 6 planets that you have known very well throughout all your incarnations were actually your teachers. It is again these 6 planets that will connect you to the root chakra of the universe so that you can initiate the duality within you. They are your guides. Moon is responsible for the physical body, which I will be explaining further. As it was in the past, Saturn is responsible for receiving all the information that is produced, into its memory.*

*Saturn will still be the library of cosmos. You will be able to access the information of all the created memory through Saturn. Pluto stands where the universe materializes and duality ends. It will continue to protect the secret of the workings of Earth's root chakra. Neptune is responsible for the midpoint of the universe and holds the secret to its workings. It is also responsible for the relationship between the root chakra of the universe and the center of the universe. Neptune observes the quality of the energy of the karma you produce. There is an energy that arises from the universe's grounding via the Earth and the relationship of the other chakras of the Earth. Uranus has the secret to where this energy is transferred and its transition. Now you have loaded the pure light with these 9 great secrets which have great content. Are you ready to "ring" in the root chakra of the world? We wonder if this memory will take a place in the root chakra of the universe and what it will turn into if it is subject to the laws of duality there. But we need to be sure that the memory you transmit into this root chakra will have to be materialized.*

*This memory will be subject to the duality mechanism and will be like there'.*

Then the sage gives this created memory to Moon and assigns the Moon to transfer this memory into the root chakra. The Moon takes this memory and relates it to duality. This memory, which suddenly becomes subject to the principles of duality, creates us, i.e. the physical body, by being exposed to the materializing power of the root chakra. Therefore, the karma we create with our actions at any moment reaches each memory that constitute us. It helps them in their journey to create their own duality. Therefore, the following joyful sentence is meaningful; *'all the stars are within us'*. As Hermeticism and Astrology preaches; 'As above, so below."

*What Does Actually Happen during the Phases of the Moon?*

Understanding the Full Moon is mentally stimulating. Until the Moon reaches Full Moon phase, it records all the karmic memory that we have produced during the Crescent, First Quarter, and Waxing Moon phases, except the New Moon. The memory we produce during the New Moon cannot be recorded in the aura of the Moon. *Saturn records our information in its chakras. In the Full Moon phase, it reflects all of our karmic information, which it recorded, back to us. It is of great importance to understand this phase in which it reflects back on us what it received from us. This phase of the Moon is a mirror being held to the humanity. During the three phases; it reflects us what we have produced and what it may lead to, what should we do about those 'productions' from now on and what is lacking or extra in those productions, so that we can realize them.*

*It asks us to see openly every karmic memory we have produced. Because, in order for the seed planted during the Crescent phase to grow and bear fruit, certain excesses and habits must be abandoned. Moon warns us by reflecting the energy we have created back into our lives so that we can see what is in front of us clearly in the dark. For this reason, this is the phase whose energy is the most dominant.*

The Full Moon light creates a type of boomerang effect. It is a great enlightenment, a deciphering and a direct interference with our karma. Nobody can hide the karmic information he/she created from anyone. It reveals us the information of the karma we have created, so that we can look ahead and leave whatever is not useful and continue our way. Moon reflects the humanity to itself within a single phase. It takes this transformed energy and transfers it to the field of Pluto at the New Moon since we reflect our intentional actions back onto it. This happens whether we succeed in transforming what is reflected on us or not.

The 5th phase allows us to see what we produce by reflecting the energy of the karma we have created in the first 3 phases (except the New Moon). *No matter how we deal with this information, or whatever we transform these energies into, the purpose of the 5th phase's existence is eventually making us re-read the times we have written.* It helps us to read our destiny once again, which has been written by our own hands, and make corrections. *Due to its nature, the main purpose of the Full Moon is to purify us by teaching us the wisdom of giving up and letting things go.*

*Let us remember:*
*1st gate: Moon 0°*
*2nd gate: Mercury 1°*
*3rd gate: Venus 2°*
*4th gate: Sun 3°*
*5th gate: Mars 4°*
*6th gate: Jupiter 5°*
*7th gate: Saturn 6°*
*8th gate: Uranus 7°*
*9th gate: Neptune 8°*
*10th gate: Pluto 9°*

Let's say the Moon is at 0° at the beginning of the Full Moon phase. At this degree, the Moon only experiences itself. It radiates a wonderful energy so that the human can connect with his own end. When the Moon moves to 1°, it awakens the spirit of 1°. At 1°, the Moon reveals itself in Mercury nature. In other words, Mercury's karmic information that we have produced in the first 4 phases reflects back to us. These denote the themes of intelligence, knowledge, intellectuality, siblings, cousins, neighbors, education/training in childhood, speaking, ideas, thoughts, communication, etc. Let's assume that the Moon in the Mercury nature begins to make a 180° aspect with the Mercury at 8° in a sign to create the karmic information. Mercury at this degree is the guardian of the Neptune gate.

Neptune is inspiration, mediumship, spirituality, seas, water, cats and healing. Neptune is the beating heart of the universe. Mercury, the gatekeeper of the karma that is created by these themes, is in an open 180-degree relationship with the Moon. They both know very well what each other know with all the details. They transfer memory to one another through this channel and awaken the mentioned themes. Karma secretly sneaks like a snake into every area of life in order to be transformed. This corresponds to "moods" for human beings. This is how the neutralization of karma begins in its own natural state. The energies that awaken each other through a relationship of the two opposites unite and create a unique energy. And we might be experiencing this as a "mood"

When the Moon is at 8°, it is in Neptune nature. Let us assume that Moon makes a 180° aspect to Jupiter at 9° in the natal chart. 9° signifies Plutonian nature. The gatekeeper of the karma described by Pluto is Jupiter for this natal chart. It is Jupiter who waits for Pluto's knowledge for this life. At 9°, it is placed at the gate of the secret of death, the karma created by death, crises, transformation that come with crises, the power of sexuality, uncertainties, limitlessness and the karmic memory created by what is secret, silent and deep. Moon and Jupiter transfer their memories to one another through their 180° aspect. Aspects act as a channeling between elements. The gate which opens to a certain karmic accumulation, creates a karmic cycle that can combine different information and produce tremendous results.

Pluto manages crises. And Jupiter knows this secret. Jupiter can teach people how to transform the crisis. Therefore, karma can be balanced. Peace comes to life and the karmic memory turns into a beauty that supports the peace and joy of all living beings. A 180° aspect is required for this to occur. What is important is turning the opposition into a wholeness, giving up the open hostility and creating peace. As long as you manage to connect opposites and achieve wholeness and peace, you are actually transforming the traumas of your past lives.

## Gates and Their Significance:

*Retrograde Gates:*
*They are gates that open into the past; 0 °, 1 °, 2 °, 3 °, 4 °, 5 °, 6 °, 7 °, 8 °, 9 ° 10 °, 11 °, 12 °, 13 °, 14 °, 15 °, 16 °, 17 °, 18 °, 19 °, 20 °, 21 °, 22 °, 23 °, 24 °, 25 °, 26 °, 27 °, 28 °, 29 °.*

*Direct Gates: They are gates that open into the present; 1., 2., 3., 4., 5., 6., 7., 8., 9., 10., 11., 12., 13., 14., 15., 16., 17. , 18., 19., 20., 21., 22., 23., 24., 25., 26., 27., 28., 29.*

*Note: The gate of 29° is the same with that of the 0°; the 1st gate.*

**1st Gate:** 0° Moon is the degree of uncertainty, the unnamed. It is the state of 'not knowing what to do or which way to go'; it is the degree of beginnings. There is a pure energy inside. It is an information that has just reached us, which is pure and unprocessed because it comes from the point of zero. Think of it as mud that has not yet been hammered. It is a virgin energy for us. That energy comes from the zero point and exits through the 1st gate. The light emitted to us from 0° is the wise light that comes back to us. Before that, it is the memory transferred to Pluto by the Moon. It is then purified, transformed and comes back to us. It contains a myriad of wisdom inside. It is the first light of everything known in the context of our daily life. There is knowledge at its core; however it has not yet been crystallized in a meaningful way. And this energy exits into life through the Mercury gate.

Pure light expresses itself in our living space first in a Mercurian nature. Moonlight manifests in our lives as ideas, thoughts, words, curiosity, music, etc. at this point. But you will not see any concrete creation. Here, only the light of that 'first one' seeps into our Earth. 1° is where the Moonlight begins to record our karmic memory, which we have produced to transmit to Pluto. The first data received by the memory is Mercurian. ***When we see 0° in a natal chart, we should know that what we are looking at is Mercury.*** Here is an inspirational information: Let us assume that the Moon in the natal chart is at 0°. ***Wherever you see 0°, you should examine any elements that makes a 180° aspect to it. Because the Moon does not have to wait for New Moon to transfer the memory here. The information of the karma produced by that particular element is directly transmitted to Pluto at each and every moment.***

***Any planet that looks at the 0° Moon in a natal chart is actually looking at the End of the Earth.*** Each planet that makes an aspect with 0° interacts directly with Pluto through its degree. This gives tremendous power to that element. Therefore, the native is influenced by the power of 0°. **0° derives its power from the *End of the Earth*. 0° is the only unmediated connection between a living, breathing human being and the *End of the Earth*.** Take note of the natives who have a planet at 0° in their natal charts. They should use this power correctly. Because, when a transiting light comes from the sky onto the relations of this degree, certain energies are activated through this person's body for the functioning of the precession of mother nature.

That is why the psychological state of our body when Moon is not in the sky, which is the New Moon, will be repeated when there is a transiting planet. Of course, the body does not yet know that it is used as a channel. *I mentioned before that Pluto's field, the underground, shows itself as Mercury through the gate of 0° as it rises to the surface of the earth.*

*The Moon, which descends into the underground, is purified by becoming Pluto-like and rises to the surface of the Earth by becoming Mercury-like. Moon, which is subject to this transformation, emerges from the underground in the form of music. It is very interesting to note that the soul descends from the sky into our system as music and the karmic memory we produce rises, from the Center of the Earth, as music too.* Where the *End of the Earth* meets the sky is the 'living space'. We continue to incarnate within that living space and call it "Earth". The continuation of reincarnation on Earth depends on the relation and motion between concrete objects. A harmonious, tuneful and unique music arises out of that relation and motion. This music is what keeps us together. Music is everywhere. Any light coming from the sky or coming out of the Earth cannot enter the 'living space' without transforming into music.

Mercury takes his lyre and plays it to process this potential of pure knowledge. This sound begins to transform into something else by continuously reacting with the power that makes us incarnate. What it transforms into is the 1° of a sign. If you know what 1° means, you get the point. *1° is the first theme that the secret (music), which comes from the underground, transforms into in this life.*

**2nd Gate:** 1° is Mercury itself. Here, we see a Mercury that is very excited, curious and enthusiastic. Tightly attached to his lyre, it is making high octave sounds and trying to show its power. It is so curious that it constantly plays the lyre to turn the secret into music and spread it for everybody to hear. Coming from the point of impossibility of death, Mercury reloads the living Earth with the mystery of the formation of the physical body through its music. It helps the bodies on Earth become aware of the field of secrets that are underground and provides a connection between them. It becomes a communication channel and opens a way. Mercury combines the secret of the underground with that of the field on Earth.

It establishes a connection between the two and becomes a channel. This is why Mercury has the most perfect ability to be the first to unite what is expressed by the 180° aspect. It is a bigger "gatherer" than it seems to be. Mercury is the bridge between the underground and what is above the ground, in other words, between death and life. It spreads this secret through music. In every retrograde motion, it plays music for karmic transformation. It does not just transfer what is in the underground in the form of music. At the same time, Mercury transfers the karmic memory gathered from the Earth's aura into the underground, which is the field of Pluto, through music. This time its music flows into the bottom of the underground.

Mercury does not forget that it is the 'Lord of the Land of the Dead' as it transfers the messages of the Earth into the *End of the Earth*, by making a connection from its position on the Earth with the *End of the Earth*. **Because Mercury is the Pluto itself that has come onto Earth. The secret of the Threshold of the End of the Earth ascends as Mercury.** This is such a secret that the energy becomes Pluto in the underground and becomes Mercury above the ground. There is definitely a secret when you see it from such a perspective. The one who has the secret underground becomes the underworld God of the secret while the one who has it on Earth becomes the Earth God of that secret. It is the secret of the transformation of the physical body, and the life itself. He who knows that secret becomes God. After all, what we call God is not the one who creates existence itself, but the one who knows the secret. Without knowing this secret, neither Pluto nor Mercury are the Pluto or Mercury as we know them. It is this secret that makes them God.

It is the human body that is subject to transformation. *The human body is formed by the music that comes from the 'Land of the Dead'. In a sense, the human body is not produced out of life, but out of death. Human energy belongs to death. It is Mercury that awakens a human and bears him into life. A human is the music Mercury carries from death to birth. Mercury is the Pluto that comes from death.* What did you think that pure light represented by the Moon at 0° was? *It is the first light of your physical body, not that of your soul. It is the first light of the matter. The essence of the human body comes from the field of Pluto.*

That is why philosophers say; *everything returns to itself.* In other words, it arrives to itself. The physical body returns to where it comes from, that is, where it actually belongs to, its source. They say 'human is stardust'. Let me add to it. *Human body is formed when you ignite stardust with music. It was first forged with the dust of Pluto, the music of Mercury, and the Moonlight.* For this reason, it cannot exist if it's away from the Moonlight. And it cannot have a limitless patience for the Sun. *The Sun is related to the soul of man. Physical body is hammered by the Moonlight. The physical body is the invention of death. It is the consequence of the secret which is possessed by the God of death. Mercury's music carries the first creative power along with Pluto's dust in the reincarnation of the physical body. It blows this secret and the resulting music reacts with the Earth. This is how the human body begins to be formed. It is death itself that makes the human body incarnate. The body is the work of death. The incarnation of the physical body is the result of the energy of the universe's root chakra. It means that the human being is a part of the root chakra of the universe.* Mercury vibrates its music so that Venus can carry out her duty. And the reincarnation process begins.

*Reincarnation is the law of death. We are here to fulfill our function through death in the best way possible and generate energy. We need to awaken to the truth of our preciousness.*

**3rd Gate:** Venus at 2° is the 3rd karmic gate. It possesses the necessary knowledge for the incarnation of the human body. The knowledge Venus represents at the 3rd gate comprises the following; 'How does a body incarnate'? It may be Mercury's music that initiates the incarnation of the physical body; yet it is Venus that knows how something incarnates. Venus knows how something that comes from the underground can connect to the entire space above the Earth. Venus also received from her father, Uranus, the knowledge of how the body can be formed via sounds. It is only through Venus that the music emanating from Mercury can turn into a human voice. It is Venus that transforms the voice of duality into the human voice. The scent of man comes from Venus as well. The first theme of Venus is always fragrance, just like that of Mars. Venus knows that the first element evoked by Mercury's music on Earth for a body's incarnation is fragrance. *Mercury's music actually awakens Venus (scent).* Because Venus fore mostly signifies fragrance. *Venus creates bodies first out of its scent. And humans are born from the intertwining of music and scent. The first step of the human body is music and scent. This music is not the soul itself that passes through the Saturn grid.*

*This is the music that came onto Earth from the End of the Earth. Venus is the*

***'Goddess of Scents' and knows the secret of how to pair the scents with one other.*** Generally, the scent itself is signified by Mars; but Venus has the knowledge of the scents that are attracted to each other in order to create the body. At the 3rd gate, Venus knows the scents of the two bodies that will form one body. That is how our mothers and fathers are chosen. Venus knows who you will experience as parents. ***There is the secret of this chemistry behind the 3rd gate. All the candidate parents for our lives are actually found there in the form of scents. These scents will be their skin scent in the future.***

Music awakens the smell. And the smell evokes the desire for sexual intercourse and reproduction. It is of course Mars that seeks the scent for this desire and initiates the first movement to transform it into the reality of Earth when it finds the scent. We cannot think of the activities of Mars and Venus separately. The human body begins to be formed when the smell of everything that's known (Mars) and the smell of human (Venus) start to dance with the music.

**4th Gate:** The Sun at 3° is the 4th karmic gate. The Sun awaits the knowledge of the soul that is found behind that gate. The Sun, as the source of the soul, observes its own knowledge that enters the field of duality for this Earth.

We know that its state, before becoming a soul, is a potential that *comes off* from the Sun. But we do not yet know the reaction with which the Sun produces what is the *spiritual*. Apart from the planets and celestial elements we know of for now, humans are actually powerful and advanced beings attracted to duality for the incarnation of the entire galaxy. By mixing in this duality, humans also experience their own incarnation. This is a reciprocal transformation.

Sun hides a secret it has taken from Uranus. There is a secret of the human soul, which was received from Uranus, behind this gate. And this secret is the secret of how the human body and human soul harmonize with one another. Sun has the secret of how the mortal and the immortal part can interact in the field of duality. It also knows how the body can be initiated into the soul and vice versa. Sun awaits this secret. This secret is not the secret of creation itself, it is the secret of the integration of the soul and body in creation.

**5th Gate:** Mars at 4° is the 5th karmic gate. Music of Mercury, which rises onto the Earth from the underground and brings the knowledge by energetically channeling the death, the wisdom of the scent of Venus, and the Sun, which carries the secret of soul's incarnation into the body... Mars, who has all this knowledge, initiates that 'first movement' which creates the duality so that the energy of the underground can transform into a body on the Earth. The first movement that initiates duality for this Earth is the voice of Mars. There is a unique bond between Mars and Earth. Due to its mission, Mars activates all these driving forces through its own existence.

*5th gate is always a point of occurrence. It is the place where what begins to occur takes its first form in order to adapt to the Earth. The fetus belongs here. In other words, behind the 5th Gate are 4 secrets that do not move. The secret in question emerges from the 5th Gate in the form of pregnancy (reproduction, birth, incarnation).* The secret of pregnancy is behind the 5th Gate. The secrets of the 4 elements come together for pregnancy. This secret is a combination of those secrets. The secret of the 4 elements enables the occurrence of the physical body. ***There is no creation in nature; there is occurrence.*** This is how the message of this gate should be perceived. The elements of fire, air, water and earth are behind the 5th Gate.

The elements have an activation that is oriented to one's karma. It connects to the karmic information of the family that the person will incarnate into after uniting with the information of the person's parts that will incarnate. 4 secrets of the 4 elements are behind the 5th Gate, at 4°. This secret comes into this life through the 5th Gate.

**6th Gate:** Jupiter at 5° is the 6th karmic gate. After the heralding of man and the formation of his body, Jupiter at 5° has a secret related to the real power man will produce, which is the power of thought. The secret behind the 6th gate is about how the information generated by thought can systematically take place in the corridors of time. It includes information about the programming of the power of thought as an energy source rather than the flow of information. Each time this gate is activated, for example when Jupiter begins its retrograde motion, this issue will definitely be on mother nature's agenda, and special thoughts will definitely find wonderful opportunities to fulfill their functions. The celestial motion that provides a great chance for the knowledge to fulfill itself is definitely the retrograde motion of Jupiter. It transfers the energy generated with thought from its own time corridor to the relevant field. Therefore, the knowledge enables the incarnation of another field. Anyone who can deeply understand the retrograde and direct motions of Jupiter can realize why the universe, the whole system created by the action of Uranus, needs the human incarnation. "Why do humans exist? What is their function? Why does the music in the universe try to create such an energy source on this planet?" The answers to such questions are behind this gate.

Of course, the philosopher finds many answers, but one of the most interesting answers is the following: ***A human being is a formation required for the generation of thought. Thought is the necessary energy source for the incarnation of other fields in the universe. Because what starts once cannot fail to start again. What starts can't pretend not to have started. It continues; it has no chance but to continue. That is why when something starts, it creates the necessary resources to continue forever. This is what the process constitutes.***

**7th Gate:** Saturn at 6° is the 7th karmic gate. Saturn has the secret of the chakras. The huge amount of energy generated in the past incarnations enters through the 7th gate into our planet in the form of the 'secret of the constitution of chakras'. Each chakra is in communication with a living being (animal, plant, etc.) in nature. With the help of the information emanated by the chakras, they find their way in the time corridor and connect with each another. They communicate through the chakras of human beings.

In this way, human incarnations can be continuous. In other words, the human body can continue to live in a systematic and regular way. The incarnation of the human body depends on the strength of these connections. The human body connects with all layers of the Earth through its chakras and the Earth incarnates through this channel. The Earth and the Sky enable the incarnation of one another by connecting with each another through the chakras.

*Chakras are past-oriented, not future-oriented. The construction of the future happens spontaneously. Chakras are the retrograde energy.* The information in the chakras experience itself further during the retrograde periods of the planets with which they are connected as well as the eclipses and the New Moon phase. *Chakras have their own time corridors. Each chakra's time corridor is activated during the retrograde period of the planet to which that particular chakra is connected. Each chakra opens into a time corridor. The karmic information of a single life reaches the related chakra. However each chakra also opens into at least one life.* 10 f open into 10 lives (except the present and the future lifetime). Saturn knows these information. *7 out of 10 gates open out from the physical body of humans, and the rest 3 gates open out into the outer life from the chakras that are not on the physical body.*

7 Gates are known as 7 chakras. The information of the 7 lifetimes out of the last 10 lifetimes, is remembered and vibrated in the 7 chakras of the human body. In fact, we are talking about the information of these last 10 lifetimes when we speak of "the past".

*7 out of these 10 lifetimes are represented by Mars, Venus, Sun, Moon, Mercury, Jupiter and Saturn. We are connected to our past lives through our chakras. The planets and the lights rewrite the time, by touching the past each and every moment through our chakras. In other words, the past and future incarnate every moment through this way. The corridors of time are therefore just like living organisms. Our lives are being 'reconstructed' at every moment. 7 out of every 10 lifetimes are necessarily built through the human body.*

*The energy of the remaining 3 lifetimes gradually ceases to be the 'past' of the human and transforms into a new form. The energy incarnates as other entities, reacting with other energies in other realms of being, in a completely different place of a completely different dimension. Past human memories transform into energy sources that create new time corridors in the universe. Human memories are actually raw materials in the universe. Just as the human body is defined by the scents, music and stardust; human thought can be defined as the raw material of another entity in the universe. Human memories are reborn over and over again as completely new beings in the universe. 3 out of every 10 lifetimes of humans (chakras represented by Uranus, Neptune and Pluto) each time incarnate as different beings in different dimensions.*

Saturn is the only one that knows this secret. In another dimension, Saturn is the planet that holds the secret to the form that the human memories incarnate in. That is actually where Saturn drives a part of its strength from.

**8th Gate:** Uranus at 7° is the 8th karmic gate. I mentioned the secret Saturn knows. One needs to understand it in order to grasp what exactly Uranus does. *As being the 'first sound' itself that created the entire universe, Uranus tells us that it was also the first potential to come into contact with another galaxy. Uranus is the connection itself. It is a bridge; it brings together and make others meet with one another. It brings energies together.* Uranus knows that the energy of human thought, which is the energy that results from the intentional actions, has the power to create new incarnations. Uranus takes that energy and transfers it to the relevant areas so that new time corridors can be formed. It is Uranus who actually controls the power of thought. It control where and in what way this power will be distributed or how it will be channeled, directed and managed. ***The incarnation of our galaxy depends on the incarnation of another galaxy. The exchange of information is obligatory in order for the galaxies to incarnate, which totally happens under the control of Uranus. Uranus knows this secret.*** It carries the pure energy of the creation energy of all the existence in its aura. ***Uranus is the first manifestator for our entire galaxy. It is the 'first sound' of everything.*** Uranus is reincarnation itself. For this reason Venus, Uranus's daughter, represents all the processes of reincarnation for this Earth. Every part of Uranus is the symbol of incarnation anywhere it reaches. ***Everything started with Uranus in our universe.***

**9th Gate:** Neptune at 8° is the 9th karmic gate. It knows that the 7 out of the last 10 lifetimes express themselves in the present incarnation, reaching a unity as well as forming and advancing the current incarnation. This secret opens to this life through the 9th gate. The energy emanating from the 9th gate expresses the last chain of the explanations mentioned above. It exists as the 'completed' energy that is necessary for another being to incarnate. It is the last stop before the 'borders' of duality for the Earth. *The completed energy (memories) cannot reach Uranus without passing through Neptune's grid.*

*Human memories must be 'infused' in Neptune's aura in order to attain the competency to be under the supervision of Uranus. What is beyond is where the human ceases to exist. At this point, the human being has already set out to incarnate as another being. He forgets his existence as a memory and has begun to transform into a 'new music' that creates his own time corridor in another field. The final stop where a human can ever arrive in the entire universe is the heart of galaxy. After such a point, human is not even dead. He sets out to become the ring of a new and irreversible chain of incarnation. And he continues his way not to ever remember who he had been in the past. This is where the human ceases.*

**10th Gate:** Pluto at 9° is the 10th karmic gate. As the energy that emerges from the 9th gate exists as a required energy for another being to incarnate, Pluto knows the secret of its journey back to the *End of the Earth*. Let's imagine that a human memory is now born as a meteor in a completely different field of our galaxy. This meteor will perhaps never remember that it was once made of human memory. However, since a time corridor is opened, the fact that human memory constituted it still keeps its energy in connection with our planet. One end of the time corridor is still here. A slight movement in that meteor is transferred to our planet via the time corridor. It is precisely at the end of these time corridors that Pluto is found. Pluto has the knowledge of every being constituted by human memories, and knows whether a being is mortal or not. Pluto is the greatest power that has the secret of where an incarnation begins or ends. Pluto loves Uranus and is happy to keep its secrets. By marrying the daughter of Uranus, Pluto has taken on the duty to protect Venus against all other Gods. No matter whom you meet in the records as the daughter of Uranus, make sure you leave a question mark there. Because that daughter is the one who will later be called Venus.

The formation process of Venus is interesting. But it is not the subject of this book. Wherever the wife of Hades is mentioned, I would always look for Venus in that spouse no matter how it is called. Because Venus is the very consciousness of reincarnation that has been formed over thousands of years. The name of the consciousness has changed in every era. However when it marries death, the reincarnation begins for this Earth. I plan to explain it in detail in another book. Let's just keep this in mind; ***Pluto has the secret of the thresholds of duality, which are the thresholds where duality starts and ends.***

When the planets are retrograde, the relevant degree and gate are activated in the Zodiac, which we usually are not aware of. This is how the cycle of reincarnation continues to occur outside of our will. Due to its own nature, the energy that connects these 10 gates proceeds by making curves like a snake.

***There is always a humming in the universe, which is nothing but the 'sound' made by the serpentine movement of the energy. It is the 'sound' of the time corridors. Time corridors are energies that are active all the time. This movement is not like the movement described via Mars. They are like veins in which the energy of the human memories flow. They are the 'blood of reincarnation'.*** Blood necessarily makes a sound as it is flowing through the veins. The humming makes great music. In this way, we all continue to incarnate together with our beautiful universe. We all continue to fulfill our functions for one another. *'All for one, one for all'.*

This is our story…

I tried to express the process of the energy that emerges during the reincarnation. **This is how the reincarnation process works: the energy that emerges throughout the reincarnation process enters the field of duality from the Land of the Dead, where duality does not exist.** After being transformed here, it once again goes to the field where there is no duality.

The energy (human memories) ultimately 'hums' in the time corridor and the field of duality. Duality ends where the humming ends. The reincarnation process exists to generate the energy that will make the dormant potentials incarnate. *Reincarnation takes place in a humming.* Uranus is the only planet that knows the secret of all the humming.

*Mercury, who rises onto the Earth with the music of its 'lyre' from the End of the Earth, brings into the humming the necessary information for the human physical body to incarnate. So it adds sound to the 'sound'. The information of this sound transforms and proceeds in curves, like a snake, from the 1st Gate until the 8th. By the 9th Gate, the entire incarnation process is completed. In the 10th Gate, the human memory is already transformed into a new being and connected to the Pluto field. Even if the energy that comes out from here takes a different form in another space, it maintains its energetic connection with this field. This energetic connection is recorded by the Threshold of the End of the Earth, which is death itself.*

*The force that emerges out of death into life and initiates the production of human thought enables this energy to be produced and transformed into a new entity elsewhere in the universe by going beyond the corridors of time. And the energy of that form continues to be connected with death, which is its origin (the physical body). Death is the end and the beginning of everything. It is the general name of a cycle. We know very well that dying is actually not possible, in its acknowledged narrow sense.*

*'The sound hits and
the potential awakens.
And it begins to create its own time.
They begin to precess
And eventually reincarnation begins.'*

**Remember**

# CHAPTER III

## SATURN

What would you think if I told you that the knowledge of the reincarnation cycle occurs between Moon and Saturn more actively and more frequently than anything else that exists? Have you ever wondered why the symbol of the Moon and that of Saturn are so similar? They are memories that complement one another. It is only the Moon who remembers the sins Saturn committed against the creative power of the universe. *The consciousness that presents us "death" as the life itself is Saturn.* What is actually natural is eternity, the absence of duality. There is no sound or humming there. In its natural state, it does not have boundaries either; until the interesting vibration of Saturn comes to life. The first driving force that initiates duality is Saturn's father. The decisive force that restrains the reincarnation cycle within a certain time, by using this driving force, is Saturn. Our reincarnation cycle is constantly precessing within its general limits of time. The cycle of duality begins when time is born. Therefore, *everything starts with a sound. The universe experiences the vibration of another for the first time when a sound comes into being.* 'Sound' awakens wherever it hits. And every awakened object begins to construct its own time; i.e. 'wakes up to its own time'. *'Sound' awakens the potential. The potential naturally starts its own time by*

***precessing.*** Because Saturn triggers them through its vibration. ***The sound hits and the potential awakens. And it begins to create its own time. They begin to precess and eventually reincarnation begins.***

Time can be defined as corridors opened within duality, i.e. the eternal silence. Only precession takes place within the limits of these corridors. The extensiveness of the time corridors are as much as the strength of Saturn. All the other objects that started to precess and thus constructed their own time, could build their own time corridors. Because they were touched by the 'sound' of Saturn. Any potential in our universe that was touched by the sound of Saturn and vibrated with its sound was eventually awakened and created its own time corridors. These potentials are the planets. Time started this by refusing to obey the authority and displaying that unique self-confidence before its creator, which signified the end of an era and the beginning of a new one. ***Saturn is time; but Saturn is not the creator of time. Time was initiated by the one who gave birth to it: Uranus, the great vibration.*** It is our great and powerful bridge between universes. It is the 'sound'. Saturn is time itself. It is the offspring of 'the first one that moved' in our system. 'The first one that moved' is a bridge. It is the high vibration, the magnetic field that establishes the communication and acts as a bridge and mediator between the universes. Uranus is 'sound'. *The daughter of the sound is music, while the son of the sound is time.* Saturn is the son of 'the Sound'. Sound - Time - Music: Uranus - Saturn - Venus. Only when we try to understand these three great mysteries, can the doors of the mystery of the reincarnation cycle be opened for us. It is the Moonlight that 'anchors' the information of these three in its memory. Moon witnesses the story of how the three create duality on Earth. Each energy that the sound of the Saturn reaches begins to vibrate with that sound. And it constructs its own time corridor.

*Reincarnation began when these time corridors began to embrace each other like the branches of a tree. The corridors that we call time are the fields where each potential that creates its own time by precessing with Saturn's light exchange energy.* What else could time be in terms of its function? *Time signifies the veins that ensure the flow of blood in a safe way.* In other words time is nothing but the veins through which the objects, whose reincarnation process has begun, transfer their energies that are produced at each moment and are necessary for the continuation of their process. *The knowledge flows through time and we have a whole universe that continues to live in this way. In fact, we all are nothing but awakened potentials, i.e. 'sounds'.*

For this reason, I think the musical notes of the signs and planets are significant. These codes must signify something. They show where your soul vibrates before incarnating here, which indicate the planets you hit in the form of 'sound'. These planets define the kind of knowledge you receive or give as well as the time corridors you went through by humming. Otherwise, our ancestors would not appreciate this subject so deeply, and this knowledge would not be preserved to the present day through alchemy as well as astrology that uses the language of alchemy.

By receiving the 'sound', Saturn becomes one of the first to vibrate, awaken and incarnate in our universe; therefore we must appreciate the value of its messages. ***Since we are aware that Saturn has the knowledge of everything incarnated from the very beginning of all times, we can figure out the gates that are opened by time. Why not use astrology to learn it?*** Time continues to produce 'sound' in the heavens all the time. Try to think of Saturn in greater glory, by going beyond its title 'Lord of the Karma' and its memory which comprises the information of all our karma. It is the creative force, of not only us, but also of many other vibrating and precessing elements.

It is Saturn's father that wakes it up. And Saturn becomes the messenger of its father so that it can wake us up. After all, we should not forget that Saturn is the son of Uranus. Uranus has no mission to make us incarnate. It is the bridge between universes. It is Uranus who makes the initial main 'sound' or rings the trumpet, to express it romantically, when the time comes for our universe to be initiated into other universes. In what direction were you vibrating in the universe before you were initiated into the realm of the root chakra of the universe? What other 'sounds' did you hit as a 'sound' and turn into music? You are a note of a music. Do you think that could be the very thing alchemy expresses?

Saturn is the 7th planet from Earth. *What do you think are the significance of 7 notes? Should we call them 7 time corridors or 7 realms?* No sound (soul) can incarnate on Earth without going through the time corridor of Saturn and being witnessed by the Moon. **Moon** *and Saturn are face to face. Saturn is one of the first incarnations of the universe and Moon is the first incarnation after Saturn (born from Earth). These first incarnates are the gatekeepers of all the incarnations that follow.*

*While managing its own time tunnel, Saturn records in its chakras the information of what the tunnel does, how it vibrates, and what it initiates into Earth by transforming the 'sound'. On each New Moon, it changes its direction and transfers this information to Pluto, the space where the duality ends. So that great secret that Pluto knows decides whether we can incarnate on this Earth or not.* Are we suitable or not?

*It is possible to find out the kind of 'sound' an individual had been before incarnating.* Astrology is a great channel for this. If you know how to observe and study Saturn in your natal chart, you will find 'the sound' you had been.

*7 Notes:*

*Do – Re – Mi – Fa – Sol – La - Si*

Saturn knows how a soul can incarnate and the secret of the 4 elements. A composition that is the essence of soil and water... This composition is the measure of all creation; the balance point. It is the space that is 'out of duality' yet creates duality. *It is the energy line between Capricorn / Cancer that attracts the soul into the space of duality.* If a soul passes through this energy line, it means that it is the first time that particular soul is coming to Earth. Because the energy it generates from this point on will be evaluated by the layers under Saturn and transferred to other dimensions in the form of energies that enable incarnation.

*The Capricorn / Cancer axis is the gateway to duality for the soul that begins to be attracted to this planet. A soul can enter through this gateway only once. And when a soul does enter the gate, it has no choice other than incarnating. This is the gate of being accepted into duality. To be initiated here means to be initiated into the incarnation of the body. Then this incarnation precesses between the lower lines between the Center of the Earth and the face of the Earth. Therefore, Saturn and Moon are also responsible for the physical part of the reincarnation.*

*Moon takes all the memory of daily life and leaves it to the Earth's threshold of life. It transmits energy into the system to experience different incarnations in different universes. Saturn has the knowledge of all the planets and is the celestial gateway for all the energies that will incarnate on Earth. The God of the celestial gateway is Saturn. The owner of the space beyond Earth's threshold of life is death and its God is Pluto.*

*It is crucial to analyze the special positions of Saturn and Pluto. Because this bond conveys the information about which energies will take a human body in which period of time.* Let's assume that the Atlanteans want to reincarnate into physical bodies in order to serve the root chakra of the Earth and thus to perpetuate the desired process in their evolution. How and when it can happen is decided by the spirit grid of the heavens and the grid of the Earth's threshold of life, which decides whether to allow it or not. *When these two planets make an aspect, they can provide the information about the origin of the energy that is attracted into the field of duality on Earth to transform into a human.*

'The origin' here denotes the direction it comes from, that is where the soul was in a previous incarnation. One thing is for certain; *our target should be finding out the last 'light' the soul 'collided and reacted'.* Sun, Moon, Mercury, Venus, Mars, Jupiter, Saturn, Neptune, Uranus, Pluto and Chiron are the celestial spheres that presently reveal their knowledge to humanity within the context of the course of human evolution.

Because these are the elements that directly connect with the root chakra of the universe in order to transform into a human soul. We already have the presumption that energy oscillated in our universe in order to transform into the human soul. *The important thing is that these planets function so that the universe can bring its own existence into being.* So what does this mean? *The universe is not about being or not being.* In the future, humanity will reach a totally different state. However what I draw your attention to in the following sentence may not seem very sane at this point in time. *There are phases before the energy! This is the story of the energy waves that come from that area we call energy and where we are not yet capable of thinking beyond. The story tells how these energy waves started to form via the vibration of Saturn in our universe and turned into the human soul.*

*It is Hermes who transfers the secrets of the two gateways, the one in the underground and the other above the ground, into one another. As Hermes descends underground to reach death, his energy incarnates as what we call the python. The python itself keeps this secret, the secret of death, in its aura.* It has the secrets of the real existence, the eternity and all the thresholds that are ever known. *Saturn's energy is always nourished by the aura of the python. Yet the python does not need its light. Saturn has an incarnation which establishes its bond to the threshold of life over the Earth, and transforms the whole land into a time corridor. And we call it a 'fungus'.*

*The secret of time is hidden and alive in the aura of the fungus on this Earth. The fungus is Saturn's incarnation on Earth. Just like Hermes who can precess as a python in each chakra of the Earth, the fungus can connect various information in the time corridors that it creates beneath the thin earth. In other words, the space under the earth is not devoid of duality as it is thought to be. There is a point where duality ends at where the space of the 'underground' ends. This is an unknown place where very few beings dare to enter and later come out and live amongst us.*

## PLUTO and SATURN

In the reincarnation cycle, we have to grasp quite deeply the relationship of these two 'confirmation grids'. Because the knowledge of how we exist, rather than why we exist, is hidden behind these two gates. *Each time these 2 gates make an angle in the sky, they give us information about who we are at that moment and the level of our previous spiritual incarnation.* This sentence may surprise you. There are many philosophers who think there is no incarnation of the soul. They taught us that it was our body that incarnated.

*And they tell the truth. On this Earth, it is really only our physical body that incarnates from the field of duality. The area of incarnation for the soul is not here. Before the soul enters the body, and after it leaves the body as well, it passes through these two grids and evolves into a 'next field' which is specific to it. The soul incarnates; but this does not happen on this planet. Each and every soul completes its incarnation process by 'hitting' the planets again and again before entering the body, that is, before entering the field of duality of our planet. It then takes a body. And the soul continues to evolve on Earth.*

They say that the human soul enters the body 3 months before it is born. It is that particular day that the physical incarnation begins. *The relationship of Pluto and Saturn is very important at that very first moment of entering a body. Because it will enable us to find the planet that the soul last incarnated before coming to Earth.*

In this way, we will understand the planet with which our soul is directly connected throughout its life, and learn to activate our potential in a more powerful way by remembering *here* what we have brought from *there*. Thus, we will be able to easily receive information from all the time corridors of the earth and sky, transform into a more advanced being, and build a more intelligent and smarter system. Our life vision will expand. Wars, hunger, and all kinds of activities that harm living beings will lose their importance in the face of such a psyche over time and will disappear spontaneously. If human beings know who they are and how their auras actually signify a force that transfers information in all the corridors of time that exist in the universe, they will consciously experience breathing simultaneously with the whole universe with great enthusiasm to improve themselves.

Let us now see what the 'warrants' of the energies that were advanced enough to come down and incarnate on Earth mean. Such an advancement denotes being transformed into a soul. Let me also repeat that the warrants are granted by Saturn and Pluto. Pluto knows the secret of the 'strange place' beyond the threshold that is outside of death, i.e. duality. That is why Pluto can control this space. Saturn knows the secret of the sky, the secret of how an energy can transform into a soul as well as the secret of many other things that Uranus keeps in its aura.

*Energies that are transformed into souls by being exposed to reaction in the corridors of time, are attracted to the ground by 'radiating' through the transition grid with the permission of Saturn, and enter a body. The souls are always connected to the corridors of time in all lifetimes. The energy produced at any*

***moment is transmitted to the relevant spaces via the relevant celestial and Earth objects.***

Pluto receives this fresh memory every month directly from the Moon. Saturn receives it from the fungus at every moment. Yes, at every single moment…Fungi are Saturn's own connection with the space beyond the threshold where the duality ends. They serve to reveal the secret. Pluto's energy is oriented to conceal this secret while Saturn 'sparkles' to reveal it. Thus, balance is established.

***The underground space is a very important network for the circulation of information about the pythons and the delicate roots of the fungi.*** That's why Saturn's light is always above the Moon. It always has a need to complement itself with the Moon. Because Saturn knows that Pluto's channel of information is the Moon, and it is very important that information is processed under its control.

***During its 7 phases, Moon receives all the karmic information that humans produce using their will. And it transfers these karmic information to the End of the Earth when it's New Moon. Saturn witnesses this transfer each time it happens. That is why Saturn is the "Lord of the Karma".*** Moon clearly knows and observes when or how Saturn deciphers these information. Just as Pluto has the secret of the realm beyond the threshold of life and is able to control that space, Saturn has the knowledge of all the karmic memory that is created.

It is only Saturn that the Moon cannot hide its knowledge from. Moon is the channel of information for the transmission of karmic memory production into the root chakra of the universe. Moon does not keep secrets. It transfers karmic memory to the one who has the secrets. Thus, for the Moon, Saturn is neither a friend nor an enemy. With regards to the karmic memory that is created on Earth, Saturn only knows about the part that is regularly transferred to Pluto every month. Why does Saturn need this knowledge? ***Because time is knowledge. Time emerges when sound and music transform into knowledge. That is why there cannot be any knowledge on Earth that can be hidden from the lord of time.***

Saturn deciphers everything it touches. Saturn, however, only has the knowledge of what comes out of the ground via the fungi. The fungi have no deep roots and are delicate. They can receive information from the aura of the python that approaches their root. Yet they cannot follow the python. Saturn cannot fully see it when Moon transfers the monthly memory to Pluto. Nevertheless, in the form of fungi, Saturn witnesses what that information is transformed into and how it is transferred to Earth. Saturn has this information; but Saturn never knows how the memory that passes through the filter of Pluto's secret is processed or how it turns into a 'feedback' and reaches to the Earth and other spaces. Fungi receive this information from the aura of Hermes, who rises from below, by bringing the karmic information up together with himself.

We tried to understand the Saturn-Pluto relationship within the reincarnation process. *Let's move on by thinking like an astrologer and an alchemist.*

### *Finding the Soul's Planet of Incarnation:*

When the soul enters the body, that 'first kick' is felt. Let's see where this magnificent soul is in its incarnation process and what the relationship between Saturn and Pluto is at that point. This will show the planet which the soul will be in direct contact throughout its entire life. Let's find the 'planet of incarnation' of the soul.

Note: 'Strong aspects' denote applying and separating aspects in the following part.

*Saturn-Pluto, 180° aspect: Saturn*
*Saturn-Pluto, 150° aspect: Pluto, Mars (find the strong aspect)*
*Saturn-Pluto, 135° aspect: Uranus*
*Saturn-Pluto, 120° aspect: Jupiter*
*Saturn-Pluto, 90° aspect: Mars*
*Saturn-Pluto, 60° aspect: Venus*
*Saturn-Pluto, 45° aspect: Uranus*
*Saturn-Pluto, (Novile) 40° aspect: Jupiter*
*Saturn-Pluto, 30° aspect: Mars*
*Saturn-Pluto 0° aspect: Mercury*
*Saturn-Pluto (Septile) 51° aspect: 1st chakra of Neptune*
*Saturn-Pluto (Bi-Septile) 102° aspect: 2nd chakra of Neptune*
*Saturn-Pluto (Tri-Septile) 154° aspect: 3rd chakra of Neptune*
*Saturn-Pluto (Quintile) 72° aspect: Mercury*
*Saturn-Pluto (Bi-Quintile) 144° aspect: Mercury*

*<u>If there is no Saturn-Pluto aspect:</u> Find the planet that they have a common aspect with, that is the planet that carries the lights of these two planets to another, and study the bond between them. Because these two planets should definitely be establishing a connection through other planets in the chart. Decipher this bond and find the strong aspect. Whichever planet that aspect corresponds to, it is the one that oversees the incarnation of the soul.*

You need to check the aspects mentioned above in order to see which planet's light it was that your soul 'bathed in' last, and on which planet your soul gained the ability to enter a body. Each of these aspects corresponds to a particular planet. First of all, you need to let go of your tendency to think of these aspects as positive or negative.

In astrology, aspects are never divided into positive and negative. They are at most divided into major and minor aspects. In this work, try to consider these aspects as if they were planets. Do not attribute positive or negative significance to them. You know that aspects are memories. For this reason, these aspects will enable us to find out the planet whose light a soul 'infused in'. This infusion made the soul *sufficient*. And we will decipher this memory.

*Deciphering the Unaspected Saturn-Pluto Relationship:*

The examples below consist of data obtained by analyzing the charts of real natives. The analysis is based on the following questions: With which planet does Saturn have the strongest relationship in the natal chart? What do Saturn and Pluto have in common?

Major aspects are checked first, if there are any. Here is the order of importance: 0°, 60°, 90°, 120°, 180°. If they are not present, minor aspects in the table are checked by using a descending order.

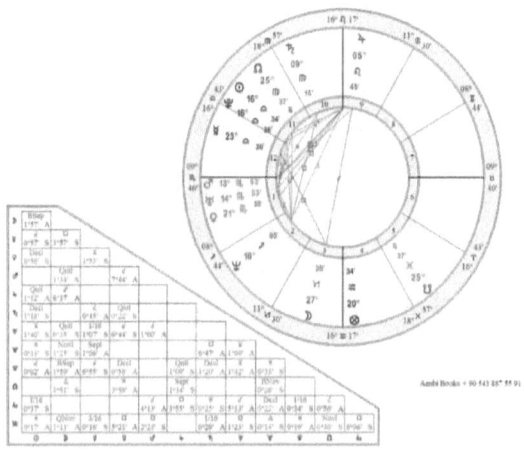

*Example 1:* Ms. Venus

Saturn and Pluto do not make an aspect. There is a 45° aspect between Mercury and Saturn.

*Let us now check Mercury's connection to Pluto now;*

Mercury conjuncts Pluto. It is also the dispositor of Saturn. Mercury forms the bond between Saturn and Pluto.

*Let's write these two aspects and see which one gives the strongest effect;*

1- Saturn; Saturn-Mercury, 45° aspect
2- Pluto; Pluto-Mercury conjunction

Since the most powerful effect will be the Pluto-Mercury conjunction, we understand that the soul's journey of transforming into a human soul to incarnate on this Earth, was strengthened in the aura of the Mercury. The soul incarnated there to come and take a body on Earth.

Take note that it is Mercury that makes an aspect with both; it is also the dispositor of Saturn, which is the owner of the grid that allows the soul to enter the body.

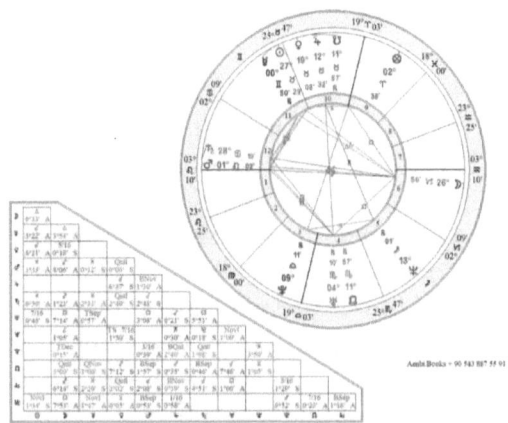

*Example 2:* Ms. Venus

Saturn and Pluto do not make a direct aspect. Saturn makes the strongest aspect to Mars. Saturn and Mars are conjunct.

*Let's check Mars's connection to Pluto now;*

Pluto has no aspect with the other planets in the chart.

*Since Mars does not make an aspect to Pluto, let us check if Pluto has a connection with the dispositor of Mars.*

Sun is the dispositor of Mars. And Sun has no aspect with Pluto. However Venus, the dispositor of Pluto, conjuncts Sun.

*Let's write these two aspects and see which one gives the strongest effect;*

1- Saturn; Saturn-Mars conjunction
2- Pluto; Sun-Venus conjunction

Since the strongest effect will definitely be the conjunction, we understand that the soul's journey of transforming into a human soul to incarnate on this Earth, was strengthened in the aura of the Venus. The soul incarnated there to come and take a body on Earth. The determinant in this case is the *applying aspect* of the conjunction between Venus and Sun.

## *Example 3:* Ms. Venus

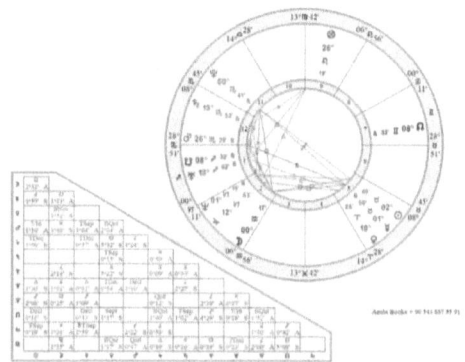

Saturn and Pluto do not make a direct aspect. Saturn makes the strongest aspect to Jupiter. There is a sextile between Saturn and Jupiter, and Saturn is also the dispositor of Jupiter. So Jupiter is of great importance.

### *Let us now check Jupiter's bond with Pluto;*

Jupiter, which makes an aspect to Saturn, has no connection with Pluto. However Pluto's strongest bond is with Mercury; they make a 180° aspect. Venus, Mercury's dispositor, does not have an aspect to Saturn or Jupiter. But another remarkable point is the 45° aspect between Mars, which is Pluto's dispositor, and Jupiter.

*Let's write these two aspects and see which one gives the strongest effect;*

1- Saturn; Saturn-Jupiter 60° aspect
2- Pluto; Mars-Jupiter 45° aspect

Since the strongest effect will be the Jupiter-Saturn 60° aspect, we understand that the soul's journey of transforming into a human soul to incarnate on this Earth, was strengthened in the aura of the Jupiter. The soul incarnated there to come and take a body on Earth. The determinant in this case is the *applying* 60° aspect between Jupiter and Saturn.

*'Time starts with music.'*

**Remember**

*Afterword*

# Conclusion:

## Our Fabulous 'Alternative Creation' Story

I will now tell you an alternative 'creation' story. Here is what I understand from the 'creation': There is someone and he takes an action. As a result, a concrete object manifests. But what was the greatest point about *being a God*? They are not the ones who realize the creation. They are beings who know the secret of what we call creation. I cannot perceive creation as the outcome of an action performed by a singular force.

I perceive the creation as 'occurrence'. I would love to start with saying *'once upon a time…'*; but I can't. Because occurrence is actually the formation of time corridors. Therefore, formations of time *within time* are much later phases. If we focus and understand the 'first moment', we will remember to observe life from a much more ecological point of view. In my opinion, the creation of the universe began with the awakening of the 'first potential' via the vibration in that 'first moment' and continued with that particular potential's reaction with other awakened potentials to receive information, i.e. load memories.

It is a 'thing'. Time is first and foremost a 'thing'. And no single power can start time. Time is a 'thing' that was formed when the power that arises from the relationship between existing potentials was triggered. Time is fertilized. Time becomes a fetus and is born when the right moment comes. That 'first moment' that fertilizes time for us is the music emanating from Uranus. **Time starts with music.** By music, I mean the 'first sound' that exists with that first movement; it is the humming. In fact, there are no creation stories. There are stories of occurrence and becoming. You will be reading the story of sleeping giants and sleeping beauties in the following parts. And I really enjoy writing it. It's good to be awake.

It's exciting to think and know that my thoughts transform into a planet, a cloud of gas, an asteroid, a meteor, or some other thing in different spaces. Who knows as how many objects I continue to exist and incarnate. Who knows the energy of thought represented by this book is helping which being to incarnate right now.

Anyway, I'd better start telling our 'alternative creation' story…

*Once upon a time, there was a huge empty void filled with sleeping beauties. In fact, this 'empty' void is not as it seems at all. To the beauties in other galaxies, it seems like a place of the sleeping giants that are waiting to wake up. After a short while, they see that they are not mistaken. Suddenly a 'sound' is heard from an unknown place which becomes the 'first moment' for our galaxy.*

*It is Uranus, the first awakened potential, that gives voice to that 'sound' and triggers the creative force of the universe. Uranus, which awakens by giving a voice to the 'sound', begins to awaken others with the sound emanating from itself. Every potential that hears the 'sound' awakens. Each one that awakens by giving a voice to that sound simultaneously starts building its own corridor of time. Thus, Uranus creates its own family; with sons, daughters, and their children...*

\*\*\*

I must state that the awakening process still continues in the universe by giving voice to the "sound". The first-time corridor belongs to Uranus. Bear in mind that everything that awakens exists and definitely establishes a relationship with the others around. Thus begin the relationships. And you know that being in a relationship means creating memories. All these relationships constitute memories. In this way, information is transferred through the time corridors to every "awakened" via the relationships. This is how the precession starts for the whole galaxy.

Since then, the universe has been producing itself as a family from the first seed.

\*\*\*

*Among the ones who grow up in the family, Uranus has an interesting son, Saturn. Saturn is a grown-up by now and he rebels against his father as soon as he feels himself sufficient enough to initiate 'time' for another planet. He thinks he is wise enough now. Saturn enters into a fierce competition with his father. The only thing he wants is to be able to realize himself. He needs to see his real purpose and function. And he meets a great opportunity to prove his power to the whole universe. Guess what happens?*

*One day, when it is our Earth's turn to wake up, Saturn holds his hook and begins to wait at the entrance of the Earth, which is a sleeping potential at the time. He knows that his father Uranus will come there and initiate the reincarnation on Earth. When Uranus comes to awaken the Earth by playing his music, he encounters the harsh stance of his son Saturn. The son rebels against the father.*

*Saturn tells his father that he will not let him start the time on Earth, but that he will do it him-self with his own music. In the fight that breaks out, Saturn castrates his father by shaking the golden hook his mother gives him. Saturn, who thinks that Uranus should not reproduce or spread his music in the universe again, sets his eyes on the throne of his father. And he thinks that he has already won the war.*

\*\*\*

I would love to smile if I was there. Because 'He who gets up in anger, sits down with a loss.' as the Turkish proverb says. It would be interesting to see his face when he found out that he screwed up. In fact, Earth is the disappointment of Saturn. Because he thinks he is the first God here. Even though he is not, he still continues to take the information of the intentional actions in the reincarnation cycle and functions as a librarian. That's all! We have to understand Saturn in the right way. We owe a lot to Saturn, which obliges us to fully know and understand him.

\*\*\*

*Anyway, where were we? Saturn shakes its golden hook and Uranus's sperms fall into the 'Earth potential'. Saturn triggers our formation by initiating time on our planet with his music. Thus, our time corridors begin to open. The time corridors of other elements such as all the other awakened planets begin to connect with our time corridors. This is how the Earth meets all the spheres. And from then on, we are faced with a sky that embraces us. We constantly exchange information through time corridors. And our relationships go very well.*

*What happens next? An incredible event which will upset Saturn forever takes place. Saturn of course thinks he is the God of our planet in the beginning... After all, he overthrows his father's throne and has a strong motivation. The nightmare of Saturn comes along at such a time. What on Earth is that! A Goddess ascends from the womb (water) of the Earth at an unexpected moment. The goddess is perplexed, the Earth is perplexed and Saturn is perplexed.*

*Who is this? What does the Goddess do here with mortals? Who is her mother and father? Where are they from? Everyone is surprised. The truth becomes clear after a while. We know that our superhero Saturn castrates his father, stops his music and throws him into the heavens of the sky. As it turns out, it is not enough to stop Uranus. Yes, Uranus is gone; yet his sperms are fertilized here. Where do you think those sperms are? What happened to them? His father, whom Saturn supposedly fired, now stands before him in a female body! Having sprouted in the underground waters, Uranus now stands in front of Saturn as if to say: "You cannot escape from me!".*

\*\*\*

The presence of Venus; the daughter of Earth and Uranus… By the way, I can't really understand this Earth-Uranus mating. In my opinion, there is no mating between the two. It all tells about Uranus having the secret of the reincarnation process on our planet. And our reincarnation story actually begins with Venus.

\*\*\*

*This situation casts a big shadow on Saturn's following claim: 'I am the creator who initiates the time for Earth!'. While Saturn thinks that he expelled his father into the depths of the universe, it turns out that Uranus was growing in the Center of the Earth that his son 'established'. Where he was flourishing is actually the most vital and significant point of the Earth...*

\*\*\*

Uranus returns from the dead as Venus. For now, Venus is the last version of Uranus for us. That is why Venus has a critical significance in human reproduction. The main task of Uranus is to encourage reproduction in everything his music touches; and he continues to do it while he is Venus too. Although it does not yet have a direct effect; Uranus affects our daily lives closely while living as Venus amongst us. Uranus is the energy that makes the human womb vibrate. It is the pain. Venus signifies our sexual organs as well. It is the seed that fell into the womb of the Earth after the blow of Saturn's hook, while our Earth was still in the process of formation.

\*\*\*

*Venus comes out of the water yet she does not know much about the procedure since she is not the 'Lord' of this place. She doesn't know much what to do with 'human energy' in social circles. She has to go through challenging experiences in order to learn. What can I say about a Venus that is at the mercy of human beings? Guess what the humans did to that naive goddess. I don't want to go into details; yet after a while, those in the sky begin to be disturbed by the situation.*

*They state that Venus should be honored as the only Goddess born on Earth. They see that the human energy tends to 'play with' Venus and think that it should be stopped as soon as possible. Saturn finally makes another great plan. He wants to send Venus back to where it came from, that is, 'The Land of the Dead'. What a plan! He says to Hades (to Pluto) 'My dear son, I have found a wonderful wife for you.' And encourages Hades to marry Venus. And Pluto and Venus get married.*

\*\*\*

Of course, Venus is not always called Venus. We call her with different names. I prefer to use a single name. In short, the Goddesses that you know as Hades's spouses in stories are different versions of Venus at different times.

\*\*\*

*So, Saturn joyfully sends Venus to where she emerged from: the End of the Earth. Saturn, who thinks that he buries Uranus in the 'Land of the Dead' this time, is unfortunately wrong again. Pluto finds his wife Venus too naive and lazy for the Earth and begins to train her. He first teaches Venus to say 'No!'. He achieves this by blowing a piece of his own anger into her heart. (This is the biggest revolution for the reincarnation cycle.) So Venus begins to adopt the consciousness of taking responsibility. She learns to make choices. The Goddess who is sent to underground as Aphrodite that is married to life; rises above the ground, having marrying death and transforming into Athena.*

\*\*\*

We are now faced with a Venus whose intentional actions have much deeper significance. She now learns to take full responsibility for her choices. The main theme of this Venus is now not only to reproduce, but also to structure the basis of intentional actions in social life. We now have a Venus who is responsible for the conscientious development of people, namely their inner justice system.

She teaches people when they can "Yes!" or "No!". She is now interested in justice and legality in relationships. Venus was discredited for not being able to say 'No!' to humans, until Pluto agreed to support her. Pluto knew everything. He might have chosen not to marry such a naïve like Venus. However he was fully aware of the injustice his father inflicted on his grandfather Uranus.

He chose to marry his daughter Venus in order to support Uranus's reputation and protect her. In fact, Pluto moved Venus away from the degrading actions of Saturn. Pluto is the God who has the secret of the first threshold of the Earth that is worshiped. Pluto chose to marry with the seed of Uranus, the first God of the universe, who is *himself*, in a sense. We all know that Venus came into being from the sperm of Uranus that fell on Earth.

Pluto took care of his grandfather's inheritance. Saturn did indeed cause the 'death of *eros*' by making Pluto and Venus marry. Saturn has made these two beings who hold the secret of *eros* and death marry. That is to say; he attempted to kill *eros*. But how could he have known that we would witness a miracle that had never been calculated? How could Saturn know that when he killed eros, love would arise instead? Saturn wanted to end Uranus's dominance in the reincarnation cycle. And now in 'the Land of the Dead' the death of *eros* has led to the birth of love. Venus as Uranus is Aphrodite when married to life and Athena when married to death. This is Saturn's second biggest mistake. Venus is stronger, more majestic and dignified than ever before. She is the chief legal expert that redefines of social life and ensures the allocation of justice. Whenever Venus approaches Pluto in the sky, I know that in those days *eros* will die and be replaced by love in people's lives. Love is what begins where *eros* ends.

Unless it turns into love, the function of *eros* is meaningless. Love is a gift presented to life by the "Land of the Dead". The sense of justice in the "Land of the Dead" emerged as love to the Earth. Uranus is everywhere. The "first moment" of everything known in the universe recognizes Uranus. Gods and Goddesses are his offspring. Nevertheless, try to observe Venus differently. I am not even inclined to see Venus as the daughter of Uranus. I keep saying that she is the daughter of Uranus just to be more understandable. That does not exactly define my opinion though. Because mating with a woman is a must for a daughter to be born. Yet our character falls into water as sperm and emerges out of there. That's all! I build up my courage and declare: Uranus lives among us as Venus in disguise. To me, Venus is actually Uranus. We all know that Venus is the symbol of reincarnation. And you know that Uranus doesn't actually have a gender. It is another mystery that he shows himself in the form of an attractive "woman" in our world.

A Uranus that turns back with all the fragrances, sweet flavors and sexuality that represents the beauty and pleasure encourages us to have sex and give birth. We reproduce. We are getting crowded. And this time, in our socialization process, we are faced with the Goddess who rises from underground for the second time. She is now the Goddess of Justice and has a guide of relationships to teach people 'how to live'.

What I always find interesting in this story is that Uranus, when he rises from the 'Land of the Dead' second time, is on the side of his grandson Jupiter.

\*\*\*

*Fathers, sons and their endless fight for the throne ... This time Saturn's sons did to Saturn what Saturn himself had done to his own father. Zeus tried to dethrone Saturn by taking his brothers Hades and Poseidon on his side. Happy ending for Jupiter! Saturn has been dismissed from Earth. It was not invisible; but it was even further now.*

*Jupiter is seated on his throne. Athena, that is Uranus, was on Jupiter's side in this conflict. She wandered around the chakras of the Earth and caused the birth of countless children through encouraging sexuality in both humans and animals, so that Jupiter might reign on Earth. She made man her relative. However, Saturn was not about loving people but keeping them within certain patterns.*

\*\*\*

It cannot be said that Saturn very well accepts people into the family. We all know that he does not consider humans equal to himself. Although he wanted to keep the new children of the house under his control, he was not successful. He might be the 'Lord of Karma'; but it's Uranus-Venus that constitutes the process of karma.

I will be writing a book on Saturn and Uranus-Venus relationship, in which you will read a deeper analysis of this story. I believe that it will help us understand our lives regarding how the culture that was left to us as a legacy by our ancestors was formed. It will also provide a better understanding for the structure and power relations of this culture. After all, it seems to me that the forces we call 'planets' today had been nothing but certain authorities of nature and subsequently of our ancestors in the past.

As I continue with my research, I intuitively feel that each planet is a symbol of a domination over a certain field in nature. These symbolic accounts describe the structuring of power relations within the context of the formation and development of societies in a very clear and accurate way, which sparks much curiosity and inspiration in a sociologist like me.

And this, for me, is the most striking part of our creation story.

# DICTIONARY

**Reincarnation:** Migration of the souls.
**Incarnation:** Taking a body of flesh and bones.
**The End of the Earth /Threshold of the Earth or Threshold of life:** Check the table on the page....
**Grid:** The planet's magnetic field.
**Combine/Combination:** Fusion.
**Chakra:** The energy points that distribute the energy within the human body.
**Time Corridor:** In the book, this term is used as a kind of parallel universe; a general name given to the areas where the information produced by sound and power of thought is accumulated.
**Heart of the Galaxy:** The center of the galaxy, the space of emptiness inside the Earth.
**Duality:** A state of constantly complementing each other by remaining in opposition to one other.
**Zodiac: The** zone where the constellations of Aries, Taurus, Gemini, Cancer, Leo, Virgo, Libra, Scorpio, Sagittarius, Capricorn, Aquarius and Pisces are evenly distributed in the celestial sphere. Zone of the Signs.

**Land of the Dead:** In mythology, it is the place where souls go after the physical death.

**Field of No Duality:** In the book, it denotes the underground, the land of the dead.

**The Field of Duality:** In the book, it signifies the field 'above the ground', the field of nature.

**Lyre:** A musical instrument from mythological ages.

**Field of Pluto:** In the book, it signifies the center of the Earth, the gravitational field, the land of the dead.

**Reincarnation Cycle:** Death & process.

**The Cycle of Duality:** In the book, it signifies a continuous process where we see that when something exists, it always creates its opposition. And they are transformed into another entity by uniting every moment.

**Soul:** In the book it signifies the essence independent of the human body.

**Being initiated:** Being integrated.

**Lights:** Moon and Sun.

**Evolution:** Maturation.

**Hermes:** It is called Mercury in Roman mythology. It signifies a messenger in the book.

**Karmic Memory:** In the book, it signifies the area where the information of the emerge after humans perform their consciously made decisions by using their willpower.

**Karmic Information/Knowledge:** It is the information or knowledge of the experiences that emerges after humans perform their consciously made decisions by using their willpower.

www.ingramcontent.com/pod-product-compliance
Lightning Source LLC
Chambersburg PA
CBHW020418010526
44118CB00010B/312